HE DID IT FOR ME

Marie Abruzzo

HE DID IT FOR ME

An Account of a
Woman's Journey from
Hard Times to Healing

Marie Abruzzo

Bladensburg, Maryland

Hardcover ISBN 978-1-957497-39-6

Published in the United States of America

First, and foremost, to God be the glory for all the things He has done, and to His only begotten Son, my Lord and Savior, Jesus Christ.

For my loving children and grandchildren and my best friend who put up with me and made this all possible. I love you all!

Contents

I cried many tears, and Jesus, You wiped them dry.

I was confused; You cleared my mind.

I sold my soul, and You bought it back for me, held me up, and gave me dignity.

You gave me strength to stand alone again, to face the world out on my own again.

Jesus, You lifted me so high that I could almost see eternity for You, and You alone knew how low I was.

You loved me so much You waited there for me, then I realized I needed You and I could never leave that love. Because I finally found someone who really cared.

You held my hand when it was cold; when I was lost, You guided me home. I am bound to You with cords of love.

You gave me hope when I was at the end and turned my lies back into truth again.

You even called me friend, and You gave me strength to stand again, to face the world on my own again by walking with Christ Jesus.

In my own strength, I could not make it.

I thank you, Jesus, for carrying me through my life.

I am no writer, just speaking from my heart about how I lived for my Lord, how before I was born, He

chose me to serve Him [Jer.1], and how the prayers of my grandparents and parents, Jesus answered. I will forever praise Him.

Foreword

I met Marie forty five years ago at the church my husband and I and our children started attending. We soon became close friends. I realized that Marie had a deep relationship with the Lord that I didn't have. I wanted that also, so I recommitted my life completely over to Jesus.

As time went on Marie shared with me about the death of her first husband, not knowing that her second husband was going to leave her. It was a very hard time for her having to raise four children on her own.

As you read her story you will see the many trials that she went through. Also, many tears were shed and many prayers lifted up. God brought her through each and every one.

I have no sister, but Marie is more than that to me. Marie has passed through the fires and come through as gold.

May this book encourage you to stay strong in the Lord, no matter what you may be going through.

Pat Saas

Introduction

This book was written for one reason and one reason only: to lift Jesus up and show the world what He did for me. What He did for me, He will do for you; just give your life to Him. It is not a religion but a relationship with Jesus as your best friend.

God the Father so loved the world that he gave his only begotten son. "And lo, a voice from heaven, saying, this is my beloved Son, in whom I am well pleased" (Matthew 3:17).

He brought me from the past to where I am today by sending people and circumstances to learn from and to teach me to become a better person to shine for Him and through Him. Through their prayers and love, they took me through many hard times.

What inspired me to write and share my life with others was reading many testimonial books that encouraged me through hard times. They showed me how to continue on, because the word says, "joy comes in the morning." As I have seen others come through, reading the Bible, I saw them come out in victory. Paul in the Bible wrote many books while he was in jail, in chains and beaten almost to death, still praising God, and touched many lives while he was in jail. I believed if Jesus did it for Paul, He could do it for me. The Bible says, "Nay, in all these things, we are more than conquerors through him that loved us" (Romans 8:37).

It is not who I am but what Jesus made of me from ashes; the flames did not consume me. I became a whole person raising four children alone. I do not go deep into all the areas of my life because I want your eyes kept on Jesus, not on problems. We all have our problems in life, but He is the problem solver.

I am learning to walk by faith, not by sight. Our flesh and emotions can fail us, but the word of God will guide us through life and enable us to make wise decisions. "Thy word is a lamp unto my feet and a light unto my path" (Psalms 119:105).

I did not use actual names, so no one would be hurt or receive any glory because glory belongs to God alone.

This book is just to let Jesus shine his light in a dark world.

Don't copy the behavior and customs of this

world, but let God transform you into a new person by changing the way you think and renewing your mind. Then, you will learn to know God's will for you, which is good and pleasing and perfect (Romans 12:2).

"But be ye doers of the word, and not hearers only, deceiving your own selves. For if any be a hearer of the word, and not a doer, he is like unto a man beholding his natural face in a glass:For he beholdeth himself, and goeth his way, and straightway forgetteth what manner of man he was. But whoso looketh into the perfect law of liberty, and continueth therein, he being not a forgetful hearer, but a doer of the work, this man shall be blessed in his deed" (James 1:22-25).

1
The Early Years

I was born on April 13, 1948, in Brooklyn, New York. Even at an early age, Satan tried to take my life or make it a living hell. I was born with bad diarrhea and was kept in the hospital for many weeks, with tubes coming out of all parts of my body. I survived, but with one eye that I could hardly see out of and very poor vision in the other.

God had a plan for my life, which was to share with others that there is hope and joy in life, no matter what life throws at us. Jesus will walk with us and guide us through as He takes care of us in all things. He has said in His word, "Before I formed thee in the belly I knew thee; and before thou camest forth of the womb I sanctified thee, and I ordained thee a prophet unto the nations" (Jeremiah 1:5).

Through sickness, health, lack of money, sad times, or happy ones, in God, we will always have a solid foundation because He watches over us as a Father.

My younger years were pleasant enough. We are Italian-Americans, middle-class, simple people. My four grandparents came from Italy; they did not speak English at all, and we liked to cook and eat. That was our way of showing love to whoever entered our home. My mom loved to cook and would feed the neighborhood. All our friends loved to eat her food; it tasted so good. All her food was bought fresh; every day, she would go to the store and purchase it. The stores in the neighborhood all knew her and our family.

At Christmas time, our church would Christmas carol all over our neighborhood and then come over to our house for hot cocoa and homemade pizza. Dad would decorate the house for Christmas and put different homemade Bible scenes in our front windows. People would come from all around our neighborhood in Brooklyn just to look at our windows. One scene was of Baby Jesus in a manger with a bright star lit up overhead, along with Mary and Joseph with the animals.

We lived in a brownstone six-unit tenement apartment. I loved it there; my school was right on my corner. All our neighbors were friendly, and everyone would help each other. We would sit outside on the stoop on hot nights and talk and share pizza, lemon ice, or cold drinks; it was such fun.

I learned to ride a bike at the age of seven, and I loved to ride up and down the city block. My bike was my older sister's, and it was a big twenty-six-inch blue bike with twenty-inch small tires on it. I was happy even though people made fun of it. I would ride that bike for hours on end.

Those early years were both happy and sad. My mother was a very depressed person, and she took it out on her family and whoever was around at the time. Once, one of my younger upstairs neighbors had a fistfight with my mom, and my mom beat her up. My mom was only four foot ten, but when she got mad, she was ten feet tall; there was no stopping her. She was so messed up, she tried to abort her own baby. She was not successful, thank God.

When her parents died, her depression grew worse. The doctor put her on medicine to help her feel better, but she turned to drinking beer and taking the medicine, which was a bad combination; it transformed her loving nature into a violent one.

She was so deep in hurt that she did not recognize how much she was hurting her children or her husband. It was hard to let go of those violent times that went on in my home and the fear that came with them. She did not get along with many people or family members anymore. I found it very sad how they did not want her around because she was very outspoken and did not care what she said and to whom she said it. None of our family members wanted us to come and visit them. I realized it, but my mom never saw it, and I was ashamed of her behavior.

The foul language, screaming, fighting, throwing things, and hitting my dad were unbearable, along with the beatings that came to us kids when she was drunk. There were five children in the household: me, two sisters, and two brothers. We would be dragged out of bed in the middle of the night by our hair and beaten. For what? We never knew. She was drunk and thought of something we should have been hit for. Thank God for my older brother. He would protect me from Mom, and she would leave me alone for a time until her next rage would come to frighten us all over again.

My mom would hide her beer all over the house so we would not know she was drinking. She was not good at hiding it because we would find them without even trying, like in the clothes hamper. We knew she was still drinking by her behavior, and she smelled of beer.

Because I was quiet, my brother always watched out for me, especially when my other brother would hit me for just walking past him. When my older brother got married, I was on my own. Boy, did I miss him, for many reasons. I loved him so much for his kind and tender love. I guess he was my hero, for he was smart and nice-looking, and I was really proud of him.

I was afraid of the hatred my mom showed to everyone—never a kind word in those times of depression. During her good times, she would give you the shirt off of her back, but when Satan took over, she would beat you silly. One night, I put my body over my youngest sister to protect her from Mom, who was on the warpath and did not care who she hit or how hard. My sister was six years younger than me, and we slept in the same bed. That night, I pushed her close to the wall and covered her little body from harm; my mom hit me instead. How I longed for a gentle mom. It was hard growing up without one, so I would go to Dad or my older sister and try to learn how to be a kind, loving person.

No one would stand up to her, but there came a time when I had to. It was hard because she was my mom, and I respected her. In an Italian family, you did not talk back to your parents.

One time, I went to visit her and clean the house for her. Well, she was drinking and started yelling at me as soon as I entered the house. I was married then with two children, and I had them with me. She was drinking already early that day and started yelling as soon as I walked in. She had bad hand trouble, wanting to raise her fist right away.

She started hitting me in front of my two children, and as I tried to get away from her, I saw my frightened children holding on to each other in the corner of the room. I had to stop this for their sake. No one in the family would say anything; they were afraid of her. She had a way of putting guilt on us by saying we did not love her. All children love their mother, whether they are bad or good, and they want to be loved back. She was well loved by her whole family, my dad the most. She would call him a cripple because he had polio in one leg. That would break my heart.

During one of her depressed moments, she had an argument with Dad. She wanted me to side with her, but I could not because she was wrong. She said if I did not agree with her, she would kill herself. I was only thirteen years old; what a thing to put on me! I carry a lot of guilt on myself to this day. When I approach someone to defend myself, I stop out of guilt, not going any further. Am I doing this for the right reason? I'd rather take the blame than hurt anyone.

Well, it was time for school, so I went. All day at school, I was worried about what was happening at home with Mom. It was hard to do my work and worry if I was going to lose my mom and never see her again. When I came home from school, she was on her bed, not moving at all. I was there alone, and she had tried to kill herself. I had to rush her to the hospital. Thank God they saved her; my heart was hurting for her, and I was so afraid. In my young mind, I could not understand what was taking place. My dad never came forth with the truth; he always protected my mom and stood by her.

She did many strange things. Sometimes, she was so drunk that she would walk the streets of the city, and we could not find her for hours. She wanted to punish us all the time. We were afraid to disagree with her; we did not know what she would do to herself or us, and no one wanted to be responsible for it. We were all afraid to say too much because we did not know what kind of mood she was in that day. We were not trying to rock the boat, so there would not be a storm that night in our home.

So, I knew that day, in Mom's kitchen, that I had to do something before something terrible happened. When she went to hit me, I grabbed her hands and pushed her against the wall. I said, "You will never hit me again, and this drinking has to stop. You are hurting everyone in the family and yourself."

I told her I would not come back again to her home unless she stopped drinking altogether. She would never see me or the children again. That time, the rest of the family backed me up and agreed because we all hurt for years over her.

Mom loved her family very much, so when she saw we meant what we said, she stopped drinking completely. What a joyful time that was in this family! What joy and peace were there, a truly growing Christian family unit for once. So many times, the holidays were ruined because of Mom's behavior—instead of joy, there was great sadness.

God had a perfect plan for us because He knew I would need my mom soon. Not long after that, my husband died. God says in His word, "For I know the thoughts that I think toward you, saith the Lord, thoughts of peace, and not of evil, to give you an expected end" (Jeremiah 29:11). It was good now; she took care of me and my children after my husband passed away. She nursed me back to health with her tender love; you would not have known this was the same woman.

She never drank again, and she and Dad had a great life serving God together. She knew Jesus as Savior, but not the Lord of her life. She knelt down beside her bed every night to pray but lived like the devil during the day. Dad sure deserved a good wife and a peaceful home after being such a patient, gentle husband to her. He was raised in a good, dedicated Christian family, and he lived the life of Christ Jesus.

Years later, I found a poem Dad wrote to his dad, which helped me understand him much better. The poem is named Father Dear.

FATHER DEAR
Father dear, I'm so glad to always say,
Your life grows better for me each day.
You're so loving, kind, and true.
I'm so glad God gave me a father like you.
Father, you helped me always to know.
God's teaching as I grow.
Your words of wisdom, love, and cheer
Always reminded me of Jesus near
Caring for me daily, every day.
Depriving yourself of your own way.
Father Dear, you've always been so meek,
It's worth it for me to repeat.
God has filled my heart with joy and love,
some day we'll meet again in Heaven above.
Father Dear, you're my bright and morning star,
I'm striving daily to be as you are.
Your wisdom, prayers, and words of praise,
will keep me for the rest of my days.
Inspired by God

I found this poem in my later years as I was going through some of his papers. It spoke to my heart of his gentle love, which he always showed the whole family and the world. No matter what happened to him, he always had a smile on his face. It is funny how I appreciate him so much more now that he is gone. I miss him very much.

Mom never really took care of herself physically; drinking and taking medication took a toll on her body. At times, her mental state would slip back to depression. Mom had many health issues and suffered a lot of pain in her later years of life. The doctors gave her pain pills to help her from suffering so much, but she became addicted to them. The doctors knew how much pain she was suffering, but they could not fix the arteries in her legs, where most of her pain came from.

They operated on her left leg. They cut it open and replaced arteries from her foot to her waist across to her hip. It was not a successful operation; the blood never flowed right, which caused a lot of pain.

In her later years, she grew closer to Jesus and could not do enough good until her last breathing minutes, even in such extreme pain. I watched her telling the nurses and doctors about Jesus. It wasn't her style of behavior. She never spoke of Him, but she truly served Him then. A nurse came over to me and said your mom wants to die talking that way. I said, "No, she wants you to get to know Jesus."

They put my mom in a room, knowing she was about to die soon. I stood with her and Dad. The rest of the family stayed down in the waiting room. She died from gangrene, which spread through her body at the end. No one wanted to be with her at that time.

A nurse came over to get me in the restroom just as my mom was taking her last breath, and she told me to talk to her because she could still hear me. I told her I loved her and it was okay to let go and go to heaven now; she had suffered enough on this earth. I would miss her a lot, but she was in pain for fifteen years from being sick. It was time for her to let go and see Jesus.

A nurse came over and hugged me and said everything was all right, that Jesus loved me, and that I did well for Mom. The family was mad at me because I signed for her to have no life support. The family started to yell at me, saying maybe the doctors could come up with a cure. I took care of her, watching her in pain and suffering. Why was I going to keep her alive for selfish reasons, worrying about how much pain she was going through every second of her life? My dad suffered just being with her daily and could not help her.

Dad and her were in my house, sleeping in my bed at this time, so I could care for them. She said to me that morning, "Take me to the hospital now. I do not want to die in your bed." Mom did not want that memory of her passing away there. She knew she was dying from gangrene, which was traveling through her body from the operation. That procedure was new to the medical field at that time. The doctors told her she had a choice to remove her leg where there was gangrene forming, or she would die. She chose heaven. The gangrene was too far gone by then anyway because she passed away two weeks later, just as it hit her lungs.

The doctors came to me later and said I did the right thing because if we brought her back, she would be in uncontrollable pain, plus she had other serious ailments. Her body was not up to handling them.

I went to the desk to ask about the nice nurse. I wanted to thank her for her encouraging words. Well, no one ever heard of her; she was not on their staff. All I knew was that when she came into the room, a great peace came with her. God must have sent an angel that night to hold us all in His arms because my dad just fell apart. I just wanted to hold him and take the pain away. I still remember to this day what that nurse looked like.

She was a small little lady with white hair and wire-rim glasses, fair skin, and a warm smile. She wore black pants, a white blouse with a bow, and a white sweater.

My heart broke to see my dad this way. He was such a gentle man. I could not console him in any way. He just wept softly in deep grief at the loss of a wife of fifty-five years. God, in his tender mercy, had to send an angel to comfort us all, but we have a greater hope to be together once more when we go to heaven.

2
Just Young

I just want to share some of my thoughts on my dad. He wrote this poem about this time.

A PRAYER FOR THOSE WHO LIVE ALONE
I live alone, Dear Lord, stay by my side
In all my daily needs.
Be thou my guide, grant me good health
for that indeed, I pray to carry on my daily work from day to day,
Keep my mind always pure, my thoughts, my every deep feeling.
Let me be kind, true, and unselfish.
In my neighbor's need.
Spare me from fire, floods, malicious tongues, and from thieves and fear, evil ones.
If sickness or accidents befall me.
Then humbly, Lord, I pray, hear thou my call.

This poem touched my heart so deeply when I read it. He sent it to me for my birthday with a card. I had kept all his poems and cards he ever sent me. How precious they are.

Shortly before my mom died, I had my parents staying with me because there was trouble in the family, and I wanted to keep my mom and dad safe. The family came to me and made me aware of the trouble. I was not sure what it was all about, but I felt it in my spirit to do this. My granddaughter was nine months old and just learning to walk. She would sit with Mom and just love on her. What a smile she put on Mom's face.

Mom would not eat for me, but my sons would make her food, and she would eat the food they made. Yes, it was a sad time, but it was good for us to be so close to her in her final days.

My parents slept in my bed, and I slept on the sofa. How great God is to take care of every detail of life to ease the pain of Mom's death. The Word says, "In all your ways acknowledge Him, And He shall direct thy paths" (Proverbs 3:7).

***

I am the fourth child out of five. I was slow in school and a quiet, shy girl. I could not compete with my sisters and brothers; they were smarter and more aggressive. Their marks in school were good. They had a determination to succeed in life, which was a challenge for me. I was timid and quiet and did not like to argue or hurt anyone. Additionally, I was always told to be careful because of my poor eyesight. I did not see as well as others, so I compensated by working with my hands, feeling things, and going slow so as not to make a mistake.

I always had to proceed with caution to do a good job in life, no matter what I was doing. This made me an extremist, so I had to learn to balance things out all the time. I think I was my own worst enemy; I made problems for myself by trying so hard. I had to learn to trust Jesus in all things. I was still a baby in Jesus, had a lot to learn, and made mistakes along the way. Good for us all that He is a patient God who is loving and knows we are made of dust.

The world can be cruel for a short, heavy girl with thick-glassed, coke bottle-like lenses. In this world, people judge us by what we look like on the outside. Mom tried her best and took me to a diet doctor to lose weight. I did, but I became obsessed with it.

I have learned in life that it is not what is on the outside of you that Jesus sees; it is your heart. He is not like the world that looks at our outward appearance and judges us by it, which is very sad. Many people are very hurt because of the way the world portrays beauty. Yet that same beautiful person can be so miserable inside and hurting. I thought I had to be hot-looking and smart, but

Jesus took me as I was and loved me. I, in turn, wanted to reach out and love others as He loved me, so they maybe would get healed inside also because I know what that hurt felt like [unlovable].

No matter how hard I tried in school, I just could not do well. All through school, I struggled to pass my subjects. And I loved school. I often thought they promoted me because the teachers felt sorry for me. I did try so hard. In the seventh grade, a very nice reading teacher took me under her wing and taught me how to read. What a joy! The world opened up to me then. It is very important to know how to read, and when I learned, I was so grateful for her to be so sweet to me.

3

Marriage

As I look back on life, I see God's hand on me. My husband did not want me to graduate high school; I was only fifteen then. He wanted to get engaged, marry me a year later, and for me to be a stay-at-home mom. I only had six months to go, and my parents did not mind, so we married and started a family right away. My mom was fifteen when she married my dad, who was four years older than her, and my husband was four years older than me. I was happy to follow that plan because I loved my husband, even though I believed in an education.

As life went on, we had our first child, a little girl. My pregnancy was fine until the end; I went into premature labor. I was walking our dog, a German Shepherd, and she was pulling me very hard along the street. My mom had said to wake her up so she would walk her, but it was so early in the morning I did not want to wake anyone up. As she pulled me along the street, my water broke. I was only 6 ½ months along, which had me and everyone else in the family concerned about the baby's safety. I held on to her for two more weeks. The doctors were very worried, and I was not allowed out of bed. Then she was born, so tiny she fit in her father's hand.

My doctor told Mom the baby was dead in me, but she did not share that with me. Thank God. I went into labor at seven months, and she came out screaming to see the world.

She was only 5 pounds, 10 ounces, and 19 inches. Just a little tiny doll. God spared her life, for He had plans for her as well.

Years later, I returned to school and received my diploma and an Associate Degree. I needed it to prove to myself I could do it.

God had other plans for me. As I sorted out my life, I stopped to ask God about His plan. After much prayer, I was led by Jesus to go to a beauty culture school; it was wonderful. I knew this was where He wanted me, around many people. I loved people and cared very deeply for them.

Even though I went to a beauty culture school at that time, I just worked for a little while. My husband was against my working; he wanted me at home with the children. But God had a plan for my future; He knew one day I would own my own shop.

I pushed my children to get a good education; that would be their future to support themselves and their families. I did not want them to be like me, with no education, because you never know what life has in store; it has a way of throwing surprises at us. I wanted them to be able to take care of themselves. I would not live forever; I wanted them to learn to be independent. My desire was to bring my children forward with integrity and wisdom in Jesus.

I was not ready to take on a family alone, and that frightened me. In that era, I was taught that the husband worked and brought in the money, and the wife took care of the home. In an Italian family, the husband is the head of the household. He supports the family, protects them, and is in charge of the bills. The wife took care of the children, house, food, and, of course, him.

The children did very well in school; I was proud of them. To this day, they have continually done well. They turned out to be good Christian adults; I give all the glory to Jesus. Sometimes, I could not help them with schoolwork or life in general, which upset me. They did very well on their own by helping each other, which caused us to become a closer-knit family. Outsiders watched us often and wanted to be part of our loving family.

Friends and neighbors would frequently come

and visit. The children had many sleepovers with their friends and cousins; no one wanted to go home. We had a happy, peaceful home with joy and love.

I realized that throughout my life, God sent people to give me confidence in myself and bring out the person He made me to be. I always felt like a loser, comparing myself to others around me. It took Him at least forty years to bring me out of my box, which I hid in from being hurt. I learned that staying in my safety box was a way of letting no one in or myself out. It kept me safe from more pain, I thought.

But there are many hurts in life. That is the part of life that I could not face. What matters is how you look at them and how much you lean on your heavenly Father for help and trust in Him. We can become bitter or better from life's problems. God allows them so that we can develop through them. If we let Him help, we will grow into His image, praying and reading His word and trusting Him to take care of us—letting go and letting God be God within us.

"Just as the great men in the Bible, Joseph, Abraham, and Moses, He teaches us all through trials. 'He will sift us as a refiner and purifier us as silver'" (Mal.3:3), yet He knows the specific amount of time that will be needed. Like a true goldsmith, God stops the fire the moment He sees His image in the glowing metal.[1]

Even to write all this down with Jesus, it took years of Him showing me to go forward with this book. I did much praying and soul searching, for I did not want to hurt anyone or remember all the painful details that occurred in my life. As His servant, I just wanted to speak the truth of God about how He helped me so I may help others. Jesus will do it for anyone; just call on Him wholeheartedly with an open heart and give your life to Him. He is waiting for your call. I grew up strong in Him and Him only. Through Jesus, I found out who I am and what I am capable of handling. One of my first prayers was asking God to make Himself so real to me that I could never deny His existence. I promised if He did, I would never stop telling the world of His great love and what He has done for me and my family. And I have kept my word to Him.

A friend sent me this on Facebook one day. It has touched my life greatly. I felt like they were writing about how I feel. Every time I read it, I cry because it touches me so deeply. I love the Lord with all my heart!

....

1 From "Steams in the Desert" by L.B. Cowman.

Who am I?
Well, that's hard to answer because, for the most part, I have no idea.
I know this: I am a simple life with an amazing God.
I am a vessel and a voice ... of Jesus, King of Kings, Lord of Lords. And the only reason worth living for is to know Him as He unveils Himself to me and Through me in a real trench life.
I have given up labels and claims.
My visions lie buried in His ability.
I am what He makes me and is making me whoever that is.
He is my life, my all, my only.
What am I?
I am His mystery-unfolding, and He holds all the knowledge of what that is and is not.
Of what that will be and how He will make Himself known in this little life. He alone sees.
I can say my goal is to know Him as He is.
And His goal is to make Himself known through me.
Only on the other side will I comprehend who I am and what I became.
For now, I'm not terribly interested.
My salvation?
Christ came for me in my twenties and taught me to walk with Him on His own turf. And for some 58 years, I have been stumbling over myself and falling into Him. I have never given Him anything worthy of having, but He has given me all His treasure.
The vision of my hopes lie buried in His ability.

I do know what my calling and purpose is: to love my God above all, with all ... then to love those to whom He gives me away. He gives all the love He asks of me.
My work of love is to hear His heart and capture His light on paper. And tell the word...

....

Only God knows what is ahead in life, for He has a perfect plan for us. Whatever happens, I had to make it on my own, with Him as my guide. He is the great counselor, provider, healer, husband, and friend, the prince of peace. My family and friends supported me with much love and prayers, and I thank them for that with all my heart. Without them, I don't believe we would have made it through. Only Jesus knows how we are hurting and lonely when we go home and close the door behind us.

But when all was said and done, I had to get up off that mat and help myself if I was ever going to make it. I have learned that during hard times, we die to self and are reborn in Jesus' image. A seed must be put in the ground to die so that a beautiful flower can come forth as my Heavenly Father.

I found Jesus when I was twenty-two years old, listening to a rock and roll radio station as we were going to smoke pot. With my friends around me, a song came on the radio, ringing out loud and clear about God's saving power. And I thought, "Amazing Grace on a rock and roll radio station?" I just sat there listening to this song.

I felt the presence of God. My friends went home, and I got down on my knees and asked Him if He is real and if He would help me understand the Bible. I had tried to read it before but did not understand the words. Jesus opened up my heart to receive His words of love.

What an amazing book it is! Jesus was always there even before I found Him; He waited patiently until I was ready.

When you open your heart to Him, Jesus truly answers you. He is there all the time, even if you have not served Him yet. He knows our tomorrows; Jesus Christ is the beginning and the end, truly the ALPHA and the OMEGA (Revelation 1:8, KJV).

He knew that I would need Him in the future more than ever. If I would accept Him as Lord and Savior, He would carry me and my children through many hurts to come.

The song *Amazing Grace* really touched my heart, and Jesus showed me that I was a sinner. He exposed my sins right before me by speaking to my heart. Then Jesus asked if I wanted to continue this way or have Him come into my heart and life, thereby becoming a new person in Him. One thing He made very clear to me was that I must go the road He has prepared for me. He called me to be like Abraham, the father of faith. I was to live by faith, not by sight. No matter what was to come, I was to trust Him, not what I saw. I did not understand all He said, but as time went on, the Holy Spirit explained His ways to me. His thoughts are not our thoughts (Isaiah 55:8-11, KJV). Every word He said was very clear, and the world around me came alive for the first time. The grass was greener, and the sky was bluer.

I did not want to live the same life anymore. I invited Him into my heart and life, and I have never regretted it to this day. He came in, cleansed me, and made me whole.

I started to grow in Him by letting go of my old self in favor of this brand-new life with Him. No more partying, smoking, or rock and roll. I did not want them anymore. I lost my desire for those things. Jesus did not make me stop them; I chose to walk away from them on my own. I changed overnight, little by little; wanting to read my Bible and go to church was my only desire. This joy was so unbelievable that I wanted to share it with the world. My children and husband saw such a great change in me. I became a better mother, wife, and daughter.

So, I gave God my life and asked Him what He wanted me to do for Him. He wanted me to touch lives with His love in my corner of the world. My friends could not understand what happened to me, and when I told them, they left me and never came to visit me again.

It did not matter because I did not have the same desires anymore; I truly was a new creature in Christ. I was in love with Jesus. My husband did not object at all. He just watched his wife change little by little into a Christian. He never said a word, for he was a quiet, loving man. As my husband watched me grow, he started to believe but had not surrendered yet.

Jesus showed me what He wanted me to be: a hairdresser. I had no money to attend hairdressing school, and a stranger loaned me money: how strange that was. He opened the way for me, and my new journey began.

At the time, I was married for five years and had two children. My husband was still searching for God. Jesus knows our hearts; we just have to let Him in when He calls, and Jesus will do the rest. So, I waited patiently for my husband to let Jesus in.

I worked part time in a beauty shop and loved it. My husband did not care for it; he would rather have had me home, so he suggested we have another baby so I would stay at home with the children.

Having another baby was fine with me. I loved children and wanted five of them. He would rather have me home with the children and have dinner ready when he got home, which I loved. He loved to walk in the door and smell the food cooking; it was his favorite time of the day.

My husband never had a close relationship with his dad, which I never understood. My family was very close to each other. On Sundays, we went to my mom and dad's house for dinner and to spend the day with them. It was the grandparents' time to be with the children and spoil them. It was not so with my husband's family; we were never invited to come and have dinner with them, not even on holidays. We would just visit on Christmas and exchange gifts.

My husband's father was always distant with me; he always had strong feelings against me. My husband was not happy with the situation, so we stayed away from them as much as possible.

As time went on, I guess the people around me saw a big change in me. I did not smoke anymore, wear mini-skirts, or listen to rock and roll. I did not care about these things anymore. I only listened to Christian music, which I love. I just wanted to go to church, read the Bible, and serve the Lord in any way I could. Jesus did not take away my desire for these items; I just did not want the same things anymore. I just wanted to serve Him and please Him.

I was so in love with Jesus, I did not even know myself anymore. No one told me about Him or witnessed to me. Even though my dad was a Christian at that time, he just quietly prayed for me, for all his children.

Once, something touched me and stirred a desire in my heart. I went to see my nephew's baptism in water, and I asked what this all meant. I was told it is when you give your heart to Jesus you die to self. So, when you are water baptized, you are telling the world this by being submerged in water as Jesus was baptized by John the Baptist. It is a symbol of Christ's burial and resurrection. Our entrance into the water during baptism identifies us with Christ's death on the cross, His burial in the tomb, the risen Saviour, the believer's death to sin, the burial of the old life, and the resurrection to walk in the newness of life in Christ Jesus. It is a testimony to the believer's faith in the final resurrection of the dead (Romans 6:4).

Somehow, it touched me very deeply, and I did not know why. But I wanted what he had, whatever it was. I felt dirty inside, and I did not know what was happening to me. Such a wave of holiness came over me; I longed to be in His presence.

The church would not baptize me right then, so I had to wait; it was a long year for me.

Though none came with me at that time, I knew it was the right road. In my heart, I believed, "As for me and my household, we will serve the Lord," and I took that stance in my home.

As the months went on, I was trying to understand this feeling in me and see if it was real. So, one day, I went to church, and I said, "If you are real, God, take away my smoking." I knew I could not stop smoking on my own. And so, He did take it away miraculously. When the church service was over, I was leaving and put my hand in my pocketbook and found cigarettes in there. I was so set free from smoking that night that I did not remember they were mine. I carried those cigarettes for two weeks in case I needed a smoke. My husband was a smoker, and it never enticed me. It felt so good to be free of such a dirty habit. What a loving Father he is to come to me when I was sinning and give me a way out.

My Dad was a Christian for many years and was a patient man. I learned a lot from him; he left his family a great heritage in the Lord. I was a lot like him: gentle, loving, and kind. Many times, I wondered why he took so much abuse from my mom, and I would pray for him. I asked him once, and he said, "Where could I go with five children?" She was the cruelest to my dad, calling him all kinds of names and curses. Sometimes, she would hit him or throw him out of the house. At those times, he would go live with his brother, and someone in the family would talk her into taking him back again. He was a good man and loved her a lot to put up with all these problems.

My Dad came down with polio at the age of 4 years old and wore a heavy brace on his right leg all his life. He was a great and talented musician. He played the saxophone with many famous people, but you would have never known; he was not a bragger, just humble, and he never spoke about it. The many movie stars he knew, like Dean Martin, Frank Sinatra, Sammy Davis Jr., and many others, loved my Dad and teased him about the way he walked. Dean Martin would say to Dad, "You could be drunk, and nobody would suspect it." My Dad had a good sense of humor. He left a fine legacy to us kids about Jesus as we watched this man so gentle, kind, and forgiving. That is how I learned to forgive my mom and realized she did not mean to be so nasty; she was just messed up and hurting herself. Then I let go of the hurts, and Jesus healed my heart to love her once again.

It is important to know your heavenly Father and the authority He has given to us on this earth. I humbly use my life as an example, for without the guidance of the Holy Spirit and my study of the Word of God, I am certain I would not be here to share this life with my beautiful family and friends whom God has lovingly placed in my life.

My salvation occurred in my early twenties when God gave me a glimpse into glory, and my first year of salvation was absolute bliss. My children and I made new friends and thoroughly involved ourselves in church activities. We refocused our lives, developing relationships with our Lord and Saviour, Jesus Christ.

My husband and I loved our children and had a great life together. He was a good, loving husband, father, and provider. But he was the only member of my family who was not serving Jesus. He would come with us once in a while to church and ask questions about the Bible, but he never gave his heart to Jesus at that particular time. He was divided in his interests, and some of his diversions were dark and demonic in my eyes.

One Thursday morning when I was home alone, Jesus appeared to me at 11:00 am, and I had a vision where He appeared standing before me with His arms outstretched toward me. His eyes so full of love, he said, "Fear not, for I will hold you by my right hand." I was awestruck and humbled, but I didn't fully understand the meaning of this vision, being just a new Christian.

Two weeks later, my world came tumbling down. My husband just returned from a schooling that his job sent him to on the border of Calif. and Mexico.

It was Thanksgiving, and the church had a harvest gathering time with the families. My husband did not want to go, so the children and I went with my mom and dad. As we were at the church gathering, our Pastor was praying and gave a message in the Holy Spirit as she wept uncontrollably. She did not tell us what it was about until a few weeks later. She said she saw a death angel over my house, which was Jesus's way of telling me He saw all things. Her words comforted me to know He was watching over us. My husband had his own free will, and Jesus will not touch that. He wants us to serve Him because we love Him and are willing to obey Him unconditionally.

My parents drove me home from church that night, leaving us at the front door. My children ran to the front door to tell their dad about all the fun they had at the harvest party. But instead of being greeted by their loving father, they were greeted by a dead man hanging naked from the ceiling with a full-length mirror in front of him.

The screams they let out as they entered that house that night still ring in my ears to this day and bring tears to my eyes. I tried to run in after them, but a gentle hand held me back. I kept trying to enter to see what was wrong, but that gentle touch would not let me pass. Then I knew it was the Spirit of God protecting me and my unborn child—I was five months pregnant at that time—from that tragic sight.

My parents went in, saw him that way, cut him down, and called the police. They took me and the children next door to a neighbor's house. The police came and asked multitudes of questions. My mind was in a state of grief, shock, and confusion.

I can't explain the feeling in my heart when the police put crime scene tape around my house. I thought, *A crime?* All I did was go to church and leave my husband home reading. I was so afraid this tragedy would hurt my unborn baby and the kids' minds. They were so young; my daughter was six, and my son was five. I was worried about how this would affect them in the future. I watched them to see how they were all the time and constantly prayed for them. Many other Christians from all over the world also prayed for us.

The police investigation went on for six months, watching me as if I had done something wrong. They had talked to other people about me but no one told me, thank God. I do not think I could have handled it. My sister's husband suggested I get a lawyer, but I did not know why. What was going on? All I knew, my husband was gone and I missed him dearly. I did not know they thought I did it.

I did not know this, but they went to my Pastor and other people asking questions about me, which she told me about months later. I am so glad she waited to tell me, for I was hurting enough. It was bad enough what happened, but knowing I was being watched, I was mentally confused and very depressed. Sometimes, I thought I would not make it. Many of my relatives believed the same thing. God had other plans for me and my children to tell of His Glory and strength. He held us by His right hand and took us through a rough life patch.

My in-laws looked at me as if it was my fault my husband killed himself. They went to the police to inquire about what happened. The police told them the truth about the death. It was a crime of passion, they said. Dad and my brother-in-law believed it, but my mother-in-law never would. And we never had a good relationship again; she hated me after that and would curse me out whenever she visited my children. I understood her pain because I was in as much pain as she was.

When the police report was filed, the cause of death was listed as a crime of passion, an accidental death by hanging. Nevertheless, it was gruesome for all of us, and it was six months before I could go back to the house. From that moment on, a spirit of fear hit me like nothing I ever knew or wanted to know ever again.

At my husband's burial, the Marines were there. They played taps, folded the flag, and presented it to me. I was so broken that I did not allow the children to attend. I wanted them to remember the good times with their father and not him lying in a grave.

4
As the Years Went On

I did not want to ever be left alone, not even for a minute; my mom had to sit with me when I showered. I learned at that moment that there is a real devil that walks on this earth seeking whomever he could devour. I prayed at that time out of grief for God to raise my husband from the dead. But a loud, strong voice came back, "NO." The voice was so powerful that I looked around because I was standing in my mom's kitchen, wondering if anyone else had heard it. I was praying quietly before Him in the pain of my heart, and I never asked Him that question again because I knew God allowed it for His glory. The vision of Jesus standing before me was my only comfort because He truly held me by His mighty right hand.

Our neighbors and friends, even the Fire Department, came with Santa Claus on their truck. They all got together at Christmas time and sent gifts and food to the house. God just showered us with so many blessings. I was so grateful for the smile it put on the children's faces, because I was so lost in grief that I was unable to help them at that time.

I was such a new Christian with a lot to learn. I thought once you were saved, nothing bad happened to you again. This is not true; Jesus takes us through situations, good and bad. He did not say we would not have problems. Looking back, I see these things helped me grow closer to Him and stronger in life.

After his death, I had to overcome many things: fear, missing him, bills, running a household, raising the children alone, etc. What emotional turmoil I was in. I was raised to run the household, and my husband took care of paying the bills and fixing the lawn, things he said men do, like house repairs. So, we divided our chores and worked together as a unit.

So began my training of knowing God is real. To become whole again, I started my walk of faith and obedience to God's word. When I gave my heart to the Lord, I was deeply in love with Him, and my heart's desire was to do His will in my life, no matter what happened to me. I would follow Him to the end of the earth. I knew this was His plan for me and my children, so that He may be glorified. At first, I did not think this was in God's plan for me; how could it be? I thought Jesus kept us from all harm. Satan was trying to mix me up so I would get angry at God. But he was wrong; the event drew me closer to Him. It backfired on Satan, and I lifted Jesus higher instead of giving up. I glories Him as He took us through our lives.

I did not want to write this book, thinking you would see how weak I was as a person. But when we are weak, He is strong. Well, yes, I am weak; we all are weak somewhere in our life. But this book is not about me; it is about how God took one weak, broken, obedient person and worked through me so He could be glorified. He said, "Lift me up, and I will draw all men unto me."

The word says, "Confess your faults one to another, and pray one for another, that ye may be healed. The effectual fervent prayer of a righteous man availeth much" (James 5:16, KJV).

I could not go back to the home my husband died in, so the children and I went to live with my parents in their apartment for six months. Someone told the landlord about it. The landlord got very angry at my parents because I was living there with them, and he told them to leave his apartment. There was nowhere to go but back to my own house. This was in God's plan for me so I could overcome my fears and face them with the strength Jesus gave me. I was so fearful, and I could not trust life anymore. I learned what Satan could do to a person who does not turn his life over to God. I was so insecure and felt as if the rug of life had been pulled out from under me. I could not put the pieces of the puzzle together. I had to wait for Jesus to help me understand His ways, not mine, and I had to trust Him blindly. I was so young in Jesus and in life; I was only 25 years old with two children and a third one on the way. I could not believe that He would let this happen to me and the children. Satan would tell me lies such as, "If Jesus really loved you, would He let this happen to you?"

I was hurting so bad and felt so alone in this situation. I did not know what to do and who to listen to. Many people had a lot to say; what was the truth, only Jesus knew.

These feelings of fear and confusion were not of God. Satan was trying to destroy me. Then, where would my children be without either parent? I was starting my way to wholeness, which was a fight every day. My poor parents saw their daughter dealing with such tragedy as they watched me go on in life.

The first time I was left alone in the house, I had to face the fear that was trying to overtake me. I had to face my fear alone, and I felt panic overwhelming me. I cried out to Jesus to help me make it through. It was a terrible feeling, like I was losing my mind. I never want to have that feeling again.

I had to face my fears one step at a time. So, I took life one day at a time; it was much easier to not look too far ahead. Only Jesus knew what tomorrow would bring, and He would take us through, completely.

When I was fearful in a room, I would go clean it to face my fear until I overcame my fear. There were times when I would walk next to the area where he died in the house, and fear would overtake me. I felt like I was losing my mind. The word says to "fear not for I am with you." I would keep saying it repeatedly until the fear would stop and peace finally came. The word also says that Jesus gives us a sound mind. What a mighty God we serve! He is so loving, kind, and long-suffering, waiting for us to use the authority He has given us.

Death was fearful to me because this man was my husband, the man I loved, and the father of my children. What in the world was going through his mind to do such a thing as playing with your life that way? In my wildest dreams, I never thought he would do that. But many years later, I remembered he told me about something that went on in the club he belonged to and that something like this had taken place. I should have talked to him more about it back then, but I just could not wrap my head around something so evil. I loved him so much, and it hurt very deeply to have this happen in our family. I was so afraid and ashamed, not knowing what my family and friends were thinking. My children will have to live with this memory for the rest of their lives.

I had gotten very depressed and could not eat or sleep. My family was worried because I was five months pregnant. I did not want to be left alone for a minute. One of the family had to be with me at all times. It took six months before I would even let them drive by my house; the hurt was so bad. I knew I had to overcome this for my own life or forever be messed up. I wanted victory over these feelings for my children and family so they could stop worrying about me. I wanted to feel better and let people see how great my God is. Everyone kept on praying for me to be whole again, and I knew Jesus would answer these prayers in His time. Many prayers went up for me; people did not think I was going to make it through this tragic event.

I was hurting so badly and did not understand how this could happen. I did not want to leave my house or go outside; that is how fear was taking over. Once, I went to see Disney on Ice and had a panic attack; I just wanted to run home. It was such a bad feeling, and I was ashamed of feeling that way because I did not understand this feeling. I never experienced anything like this before. I did not know how to handle it.

One day, my aunt came over to visit me because God showed her in prayer that I did not want to leave the house anymore. She started to pray for me, and, all at once, the fear was gone. I was so thankful that she obeyed Jesus when He told her how bad I felt. God gave me another miracle, and I was so glad to be set free. What kind of mother would I have been if I could not leave my own home? How could I take care of the kids?

I had so many questions: how will I manage taking care of the children, house, money? I didn't even know how to drive, I came from Brooklyn where you did not need a car. But we moved to Long Island to raise our children.

What Satan intends for bad, Jesus turns to good. Eventually, God used this for the good of all of us. It forced me to do things I never did before and made me go out and do them so I could take care of the children. I would do anything just to take care of them.

As time went on, Jesus revealed to me what went on at his death. My Christian book was on the table; the title was "The Late Great Planet Earth." My husband was reading it and underlined passages in it. It was, "I do not know about you, but I believe everything my wife said about Jesus being real."

My husband did cry out to God and was saved at the last moment of his life. Jesus showed me by giving me a promise for seven days in a row, of Jesus as He hung on the cross saying, "Father, why has thou forsaken me?" I kept asking Jesus what this promise meant to me that came to me daily as I read the word with my dad each night. We would take a promise from a promise box, which were scripture verses on little cards. Every night, we would take a new promise and read it out loud. I would reach into the box and take a new promise from different areas of the box and still get the same promise. Jesus said what this promise meant was that my husband did cry out for Him, but it was His time to take him home to glory.

I will not know all the answers on this earth. When Heaven comes, then we will know all the unseen answers to prayer and God's long-range plan for us. I know that, through it all, I was able to speak to many women and encourage them. Some had lost husbands or loved ones and had lost hope in life. At these times, we learn to trust and rely on an infinite Father. His love is perfect to help us carry on in a full life of joy. Because we love our children, we do not give them anything harmful to play with. Our Father knows what is best for us. He will not give us more than we can bear. Many times, He carried me through, just like the poem "Footprints." When we see only one set of footprints, He is carrying us through pain and sorrow.

I was not the only person hurt by my husband's death. Both of our extended families were devastated, especially his mother. She was so grieved that when I went into the hospital to give birth to our son, she tried to take the baby and was caught running down the hospital corridor with the baby in her arms.

At this point, I was so distraught that the hospital sedated me. That was another major turning point for me; up until then, I had not taken any drugs or sedatives. I had reached the pinnacle where sedation was necessary, and they had to tie me down in my bed at the hospital. My mother-in-law was screaming at me that it was my fault that her son died. I just collapsed.

The hospital put me in a private room so I would be away from the other mothers whose husbands were visiting. At this time, the hospital called my mom to come and spend the night with me, and they discharged me from the hospital the next day, only a few hours after the baby was born.

The hospital felt it would be better for me to be at home and not around other families that were there visiting the other moms. It was so hard for me to see the husbands come and visit their new babies and bring flowers; it just crushed me because I missed mine.

Through this tragic experience and other experiences that followed, such as not wanting to stay in the same house with so many bad memories, we needed to start a new life for me and the kids. I began to realize and recognize that my heavenly Father was watching over me and truly had me by His right hand because, at that time, I was breaking down in life, being such a new Christian for about one year. I was confused, not understanding life. But Jesus said I will never leave you or forsake you and I had to rest in Him.

My sole desire was to please Him and be the best Christian, mother, and breadwinner possible while raising my children in a loving, wholesome environment. I never wanted them to feel that we were not a solid family unit, so everyone had to be home for dinner, no matter what. I held them as a family in all things. We stood together in love and faith, serving God; I tried to teach them that these problems in life made us stronger and build character.

There will always be problems in life, and we

must learn how to deal with them through Jesus as we walk in Him. I knew He would take us through. We never needed any outside counseling; all of my children are saved and love the Lord.

5

Starting a New Life

As time went on, Jesus sent a longtime friend of the family into our lives. We both loved the Lord and went to church together, and he was great with the children. He knew my husband and I very well for fifteen years. My whole family knew him, and my dad liked him very much. We were married a year later and moved into a new house to start a new life together.

The first year of our life together was wonderful, and a son was given to us. My husband was a jealous man, and this jealously drove him more and more. It became so bad that I was not allowed to answer the phone or go outside, not even to shop for food.

The next-door neighbor was a driving instructor and offered to teach me to drive. My husband was watching him talking to me by the window (I was eight months pregnant), and when I came in, he started screaming at me that he would kill me before he would let him teach me to drive.

The jealousy became so out of hand that my children were not allowed to sit next to me. I tried to work with this and show him that I loved him differently than I loved the kids but to no avail. The tension in the house was getting worse each day as his anger grew. A few times, he would raise his hands against me. In his rage, he choked me three separate times, being out of control of his feelings, and I was becoming afraid of him by then. What hurt me the most was his attitude towards my children. He said he disliked my daughter the most. He said, "She will hurt you because she hates you," so he never supported her, just the boys, which I had to go to court and fight for. Even though he legally adopted them all. Maybe he would be right, but she was still my daughter, and I had to leave that in Jesus' hands. I was their mother and had a duty to take care of them even though he said to me that he loved me but not the kids. He wanted me to go with him to dinner, on vacations, and on long weekends exclusively, without the children. He held no regard for the children, and they were unwanted and a nuisance in his eyes. I could not do that; they were my responsibility.

He visited them once and said to me after they returned from the movies, "I hate them and will never come back again to see them." I was so heartbroken, especially since one of the boys was his and the children loved him. I must say Jesus was my strength because I fell apart. I believe that when you get married, the word of God says not to divorce. My kids loved him and were very confused and hurt. They said to me, "What did you do, Mom?" How do I explain what went on? They were hurt by their real dad, and now this. I tried hard to keep a normal household as best I could, and at times, I felt lost and lonely. Even though my husband would call and cry to me about how much he loved me and did not want to go, he seemed driven by some unseen force. It was a very sad, hard time for me to try to hold things together for the kids. Jesus carried us all through. Thank You, Lord, for your wonderous love so undeserved. I love you, Jesus.

As a family, we all went to church together, and as life went on, his extended family joined our church with us. I was so happy because I believed God gave the children and me another chance for happiness. Together, we served faithfully in our church, and I committed my entire life to Jesus, but he was not so ready, and the world still enticed him.

My husband was going the wrong way from God. I thought, *Am I a religious fanatic?* I just loved Jesus so much; I often thought about how such a great love came into my life to love and serve Jesus. Only Jesus could have planted that seed of love so deep in my heart for Him. Satan was trying to destroy me with my husband by wanting me to go his way, away from Jesus. My thoughts were, *Should I lean his way so he will not leave?* I did not want him to go. I just did not know what to do; was I being a good enough wife?

As I prayed, this came before me: isn't that what Adam thought when Eve gave him the apple? He listened to her and went her way into sin. As much as my heart hurt, I knew Jesus would not be pleased. I thought, *Whom should I please?* But the Word said if the husband goes away from Him, the wife who is more godly should help him and try to keep him from the fires of hell, not to go his way but Jesus' way. God knows how hard I tried. He got romantically involved with a woman from work. His girlfriend kept on calling the house, and one day, she even came over to see his house and urged me to let him go. I was not stopping him, for this was his choice, not mine. Satan told him he would not hurt anyone, but that is a lie because we are not an island unto ourselves. Many people were hurt, including his parents, because they loved me and the children very much. They even said to me, "Do not worry;

we will take care of you. Just let him go so he will not hurt you and the children anymore," because he was pushing for a quick divorce.

But I was so heartbroken I ran from his parents because I could not be around him if he were to visit. Two times of deep hurts: a divorce and death. I could not take it, and I did not want them to see how badly I was hurting. I loved them too much for that.

Satan knew if I leaned his way, all would be lost in my soul, and sin would have moved down to my children. I could not give in to evil to satisfy him or to keep him. I thought, *Not another marriage gone; what would the kids think of me?* One day, my son came to me and blamed me for his leaving. Even when he wanted me to lie on the divorce papers, I would not because I felt in the future, it may come around and hurt me. My son asked, "What did you do?" I did not want to tell him the truth, but Jesus said to. I did not want to hurt him. How I cried! I had to tell him that he wanted only me, not the children. I did not want them to think it was their fault because that was not the truth. It was Satan trying to destroy our family. I was so happy when, one day, that same son came to me and said that my husband was just being selfish. I was so glad that God gave him the right answer.

It was around Valentine's Day, and my son bought me a dozen roses to say he was sorry for blaming me. Well, let's put a funny footnote to this event. It was very cold, and he left the flowers in his car overnight. When he gave them to me the next day, they were frozen. Frozen roses really smell bad, and we had a good laugh over it. When I opened them, he was disappointed, but I was so thankful for his thoughtfulness in buying them for me. I did not want him to hate me, and I did not want him to be hurt, but he was okay with it. I knew he loved his stepdad, and I did not want hatred to grow in his heart. Thank God!

To this day, I have a wonderful relationship with my son. He is always there for me. I think it was wise to tell him the truth because his not knowing the truth could have put a wedge between us as the years went on.

Over time, my husband grew restless and began to have divided interests, which eventually led him down the road of adultery with one of his co-workers. He decided that he wanted a divorce. He was so determined to go his own way and wanted out of the marriage. He began threatening the children and me, leaving us hurt and confused.

He would threaten to take the children and the house from me, which was a lie because he did not want the children at all, not even to visit them; he never came around. I went to my lawyer, and he said not to listen to him. I should not have listened because he told me he hated the kids and never wanted to see them again. I did not realize he was bluffing so that I would divorce him quickly. He wanted out right away. I did not understand what was happening because I believed Jesus would not let this happen. I had prayed that this marriage was of Him, and He gave me a scripture verse of Isaac looking for a wife. I prayed long and hard on this matter, and I knew the marriage was what Jesus wanted, so I put my complete trust in Him.

Jesus showed me to continue to be a good wife, no matter what my husband said or did, so I would not sin in this matter.

I still cooked his meals and washed his clothes, which seemed to make him angrier with me. He stopped supporting us and came home drunk at times. His girlfriend would come in front of my house. When I approached her outside, she remarked she wanted to see how we lived so he would give her the same kind of living. She would call my house and question the children and me. What kind of person would do such a thing? My husband's behavior was bad enough, but to be harassed by his girlfriend was hard to deal with.

He would buy her presents and leave them around the house so I would see them.

Why didn't he just leave and not torment me? He would be at the bar and call me, crying, saying how much he loved me, and the next minute, he would scream at me. I thank God for my best friend, who held me steady and talked some sense into me. She would call or come over and pray with me, which I needed a lot of. I remember a day after his crazy phone calls, I sat on my bedroom floor and just cried at his cruel words. He said, "I know why your husband killed himself; it is because of you." This was another lie of Satan to deeply hurt me.

He knew he did very wrong, and he called my girlfriend and told her to call me because he hurt me really bad this time.

No matter what I did, it did not satisfy him. He just wanted a new wife with no children. I did not understand because we had been friends for 15 years, and he knew my three children. I was so hurt and angry at life that I had no compassion for his soul at all. I was worried about how to support the children.

I came home from church one morning after the pastor preached a sermon on compassion. God spoke to me and told me I was being stubborn. He told me to have compassion for my husband (I felt my husband was being selfish). Jesus showed me that day He is the GREAT I AM, and He will take care of us. And He did without any shadow of doubt in my mind.

I prayed for my husband that Satan would not have his way and that our family would have a complete restoration. But sometimes what we think is not the best solution. God responds differently, which brings Him all the glory and praise. The affair was devastating for all of us, including his parents, who truly loved us.

I sought guidance from my pastor, who suggested that for my safety and the children, it was best for me to release him. I could not understand what was going on in my life. I married believing and knowing God was in the middle of our marriage. I could not understand what was going on because, once again, my heart was broken. I had to learn that God is a gentleman and will not go against anyone's will. Even though He died for that will, He would not make him stay with us if my husband really wanted to leave. My husband believed Satan's lies, and he listened to them. He was determined to go; there was no stopping him. I watched Satan messing up his head, and it hurt because there was nothing I could do. My husband would not listen to me, and many nights, I cried myself to sleep, wondering where he was and with whom. He was getting uncontrollable and violent, which frightened me. I did not know what he would do next. He would come home late at night, smelling like perfume and whiskey.

He would threaten me with many things. He wanted a divorce right now and wanted me to sign papers with lies on them. I would not do it because they were not the truth. That made him angry, and his dad told me to just sign them and not let him hurt me anymore. But I could not sign them. Those lies were hurtful, and I did not want my children years later to read lies about me.

He could not find a good reason to divorce me, so he made up lies. Even his lawyer said to him, "Why are you leaving her? She sounds like a great person after being married six years."

He wanted me for himself and said if I gave the children up, he would stay with me. I could not do this, for I brought them into this world. They did not ask to be born, and it was up to me to take care of them.

He was very jealous, and the kids could not even sit next to me. I was not even allowed to answer the phone. He started to take things from the house and sell them. I knew it was time; my heart could not take anymore. I had a weird dream that I was in prison, lying on a wooden bench, and a water faucet was above me, dripping on my head, torturing me. It was God revealing the truth of the situation.

During this time, I was in my prayer closet; I had a vision of my husband, and we were holding hands. Satan took him away, and I cried out to God not to let that happen; take me instead. At that moment, I was taken to a very cold place, and a loud voice said, "No, you cannot take her, but he must go." How my heart broke to know at that moment that he was going, for God was angry with him because he did not want to turn from sin. It was time to let go of him; my other half would be gone. I was husbandless again, the sole support for the children. I got discouraged at times.

In all these different experiences, we are to rely on Jesus living inside of our hearts, regardless of our feelings, as we walk obediently before Him. This is where I got into trouble. I tried to walk by my feelings, which were taking over me, not by faith. I stumbled at times, and Satan told me, "Jesus does not care about you. See all that happened to you. Where was He?"

I thought Jesus wasn't listening to me. His mercy seemed nowhere to be found. My loneliness lasted for weeks until my heavenly Father seemed to say to me, "You have been looking for Me in the outside world of EMOTION, yet all the while, I have been waiting inside for you. Meet Me now in the inner chamber of your spirit, for I AM there." How sad it was to be in this place, but here again, it was a learning experience. Now, looking back, I am thankful for it because it taught me not to look around but to stand in faith, and victory comes much sooner.

One time, I got so down that I would not get out of bed, and I cried all the time. I was so down that I prayed for something bad to happen to him. My best friend called that day and told me exactly what I said to God, and it scared me really bad knowing He heard me. God showed me I was wrong for that thought and urged me to trust Him in this matter. I felt so bad for what I said that I repented to Jesus and asked forgiveness. Praying for something bad to happen to him was the wrong thing to do, for revenge is the Lord's, not mine. I knew no weapon formed against me shall prosper; God's Word said so, even though I saw the children hurting with no father and times were so hard that I let Satan's lies hurt me so. But his lies brought me closer to my Heavenly Father because He understood my hurt.

When he left us, he never came around again and would not pay child support. He asked me if I wanted him to come around to visit the children. I said, "No, not after you said you hated them," which was just his excuse to blame me for not coming over. But if he really wanted to see them, nothing could have stopped him. I had to go to court, and the judge said his second wife wiped him out when she divorced him. He was also married two more times; how sad I was for him. We had been friends for fifteen years, and I thought I knew him, but did we really know anyone? Only Jesus knows our hearts.

As I was at such a low point, my friend took me to a special eye doctor and bought me contacts. I was told many times that because my eyes were so bad, I could not wear contacts; they would only make my eyes worse. I was so happy to take those ugly glasses off and to see so much better with the contacts. It was a tremendous sacrifice on her part because she and her husband were struggling financially, but she faithfully responded to the Lord's calling. But to me, it was the greatest gift I ever received in my life, and it was given by God through her.

Such a true friend from God. She knew all I had been through right from the start, and she was a fair judge in all things. She was tender and kind, not judgmental or hard with me. I needed an outsider to help me put things in their proper order since Satan's darts were coming from so many places.

People in the church I was close to and loved dearly seemed to unexplainably turn against me. With this, my husband leaving, family problems, and the passing of my husband years before, I was ripe for the enemy to step in and try to take my soul. I knew God would not let that happen because He is on the throne taking care of His children, and Satan has to go before him to ask permission to do that.

Eventually, peace came over me with His great love, and I thank Him for it. Because before this all happened, Jesus prepared me for it. One night, Jesus appeared to me again during this rough time in my life and woke me from a deep sleep. There was a strange storm that night. As Jesus spoke to me, He pointed at the window to the storm outside and said, "You will go through the midst of the storm, but your house shall stand because you believed in me, the Rock, the Lord Jesus Christ." He said, "You have built your house on the Rock and not on the sand, so as the storm comes, do not be dismayed; the waves will not destroy you."

The pressure of hard times makes us value life. Every time our life is spared and given back to us after a trial, it is like a new beginning in life. It seems we better understand how important it is and thereby apply ourselves more effectively for God and for people. It helps us to understand the trials of others and equips us to help them through hard times as well since we have been there already.

> *"Trials and difficult times are needed to press us forward. They work in the way the fire in the hold of a mighty steamship provides the energy that moves the pistons, turns the engine, and propels the great vessel across the sea, even when facing the wind and the waves." A.B. Simpson.*

"For we would not, brethren, have you ignorant of our trouble which came to us in Asia, that we were pressed out of measure, above strength, insomuch that we despaired even of life: But we had the sentence of death in ourselves, that we should not trust in ourselves, but in God which raiseth the dead" (2 Corinthians 1:8-9).

6
Hurt

My in-laws were great people, and we loved them very much. I knew they hurt for us and did not know what to do. But they said their son needed help and wished he had stayed with me because I could have helped him.

My husband's parents came for my birthday. As we were eating dinner, a man came to my door and served me with divorce papers. I was devastated, and my husband's parents tried to comfort me. I will always love them and his whole family.

From that day forward, he never came around or called to see how the children were. This was so sad to me. His lawyers made a mistake and sent his papers of accusation of why he wanted to divorce me. I received them by mistake, and the Lord told me to answer every allegation against me. Well, I cried like a baby because I had to expose what went on in my household, and I was ashamed. I answered to the best of my ability. Every time his parents came over, he wanted me to throw them out and would curse them so badly. I could not do that because I loved them, but he hated them. I did not understand that; they were great people. I showed the papers to my pastor, and she took them and showed them to his parents. His dad said his son was messed up and was very sad. That was just one of the things he said. I kept those papers to this day so the truth can reign. There were many silly things against me.

My girlfriend loved to read and gave me a book, "When the Pieces Don't Fit." In this book, the author talks about the many things that happened in her life and how she could not put them together. This book, written amid struggle, detailed how she turned life's tragedies into stepping stones of growth in greatness. It was a great wound healer to me and, I believe, to many other people who read it.

I was now divorced, which was unheard of in my family, and a widow with limited education and a family to support. At first, it occurred to me what would happen if I was not able to support the children; they would be taken from me. I could not bear the thought.

I prayed and asked the Lord how I could serve Him and support my family. He told me to open my own beauty shop. This shop would be Christ-centered only to glorify Him. I asked my children what we should name it. We all agreed on Miracle Hair Designs because it was a miracle we were there. But my customers thought we could do miracles, which was funny.

As I began life on my own, I had to relearn everything from a new perspective. My husband was the disciplinarian in our household, and now I had to learn to discipline. In addition, I had to make ends meet and take care of the children's needs, sicknesses, problems that come from everyday life, and whatever else that came up along the way. I was not a very aggressive person. I had to learn how to come out of my shell and to be a shop owner and a single mom. I prayed, "Jesus, please help me do this right and make the right decisions for my family."

My younger son was playing football during lunchtime at school. He was tackled to the ground and dislocated his knees. I filled out a school report and took him to the doctor. The doctor said he should be operated on and put him on crutches. As he was going from class to class, some boys fooled around with my son and said you do not need those crutches; they pulled them out from under him. He fell on the hard floors at school, which made his knee swell up like a watermelon.

I went back to his doctor the same day that this happened, and the doctor admitted him to the hospital the next morning for emergency surgery on his knee. Months later, he had to have the other knee done also because he landed on both knees with the other boy on top of him.

The school gave me such a difficult time; they did not want to pay for the operations. Jesus told me to keep fighting them on this. I was not much of a fighter, but I obeyed and stood my ground. Because if they did not pay, I did not have the money, and the doctor said if he did not get operated on, he would be in a wheelchair for the rest of his young life.

God gave me the strength to stand my ground. I had to go to the school superintendent for help, and he cursed me out and threw me out of his office. Of course, I cried, and my dad came back with me and put him in his place. They finally did pay for the operations. That was all I wanted; I had no medical insurance and no money, and I did not want to sue. My husband was to pay for medical insurance, but he never did.

He had the operation, and it was a success. The doctor was great with my son and took good care of him, for he was only thirteen years old and frightened. They let me go to the operating door with my son, and I said a prayer with him to guide the doctor's hand. The doctor also bowed his head and prayed with us.

Months later, during school activities, he was playing kickball, and he dislocated his hip. The school took him to the hospital by ambulance to the emergency room. The same doctor was passing him by and said, "Hey, what are you doing here?" and took care of him right away. It just goes to show that Jesus is with us all the time, watching over us. I thank Jesus for His help because I did not know what to do. Did he really need this operation? Is there something wrong with his body now that his hip is dislocated? This doctor took care of it all and said he was fine, just growing faster than his muscles, so their strength took over. He did sprout up very fast that year. He went from being short to six foot tall. The doctor said that was a good growing spurt that usually happens during puberty. What a relief it was for my mind to know he would be okay.

7
Moving On

Jesus knew what I needed in life, and He sent me a very special friend. She was the opposite of me but a life saver in many ways. With her gentle love, she helped me to overcome many obstacles in life. Without her, I would not have made it through all that was ahead of me. She was a good Christian and loved the Lord very much.

We held prayer meetings and saw many people saved and healed. We both loved the Word and prayed many times together, and she prayed many times for me separately. God knew I needed those prayers. My friend was a continuous pillar of support for me and my children and a tremendous inspiration to all of us. She could fix anything, which encouraged me to try even harder in whatever my struggles were and that I could do all things through Christ Jesus, so do not fear. People around us thought I was the leader in our friendship, which was not true at all. She was my backbone and kept me on the right road. I could understand what it looked like from the outside, but it was not true. Jesus sent her to our family to encourage me to go on. And I thank her and her family for their tender love. I struggled with my driving, starting my own business, dressing better with nice colors (my friend brought to my attention that I always wore black, which I did not realize—such a mourning spirit), and, most of all, believing in myself.

After all the hurt and struggle I had overcome, I truly had no self-esteem left. I had to realize that I was a child of the most high God, and everything He created was good. At times, it seemed unbelievable that I was created in His image.

This unbelief was a period I called an overwhelming hindrance, yet through the Word of God and the help of my friend, I realized more fully my identity in Christ and that I truly was a beautiful work of art designed by God. I continue to walk on the King's highway.

Her family and mine have become close friends to this day. Whenever I had to make a big decision, she and I would pray about it, and Jesus would direct our path.

I was so glad she was there; she encouraged me to go forward many times and would tell me not to bury my head in the sand. I would rather run from a problem than face it; she was the opposite of me. She gave me confidence and taught me not to be afraid and that I could do it. She would push me in the right direction and do it with me, and then when I started, she would let me go to finish the project on my own. She knew I could do it; I just needed a push. She would say we are like Jonathan and David in the Bible, which was so true.

I had never worked in a public place before, and now I had become the sole breadwinner for myself and four children. Being a hairdresser, I had to stand in front of a mirror all day long; for some unknown reason, I hated looking at myself. Oh well, it was something new to learn how to love oneself. The first time I looked at the full-length mirror at my station, I wanted to run out of there quickly. It was a new lesson in learning to love and not be ashamed of myself because if God loved me, I had no choice. He does not make junk.

I learned through trial and error that I could do all things through Christ who strengthens me, and no weapon formed against me would prosper (Isaiah 54:17, KJV). Here was another lesson I had to learn in trusting God. So I put on my whole armor of God and set forth in faith (Ephesians 6), not in fear, knowing that my God would supply all my needs according to His riches in glory.

One day, I was praying to find a good dentist in my area. I knew there had to be one close to my house, but I could not find one, no matter how hard I looked. One day, I was working at my beauty shop, which was about 20 minutes from my home. The mailman came to deliver my mail. I could not believe what I saw in my bunch of mail. Someone else's mail was mixed in with mine; it was the dentist I was looking for! How did that happen? His office was 20 minutes from my shop, and I have his mail. Well then, I knew God answered my prayers to find a good dentist nearby, and I was so happy to find him. He was not just a good dentist, but his prices were fair also, and he took good care of me. Once again, I was so thankful to Jesus for His help.

My desire was to move forward in every area, raise my children in a good Christian home, and reach the lost around me. I became a Sunday school teacher and a Missionette leader. I visited the shut-ins and the sick in the hospital. I encouraged all who would listen that God is real and alive as He uses each one of us to lend a helping hand to our neighbors and friends.

My children were just as involved in church activities as I was. Once, my son's school called and asked if he would be able to join a discussion group to help other kids with their problems. My son had a loving way about him to help people and stand up for the weak and lost. People just loved him and enjoyed being around him; Jesus was doing a work with us all. What would have happened to us if we had gone Satan's way? I would have been walking out of God's plan for me and the children.

I was coming along in life very well, trusting my Heavenly Father, but Satan was doing his work behind the scenes, trying to destroy me by lies he put in the people in my church. This caused many problems for me. I was so heartbroken because it became very hard to stay in this church that I loved so dearly; it was my second home.

At this time, God reminded me of how He called me to work for Him. I did not understand it all, but from time to time, He would reveal what He called me to do for Him. Like Jeremiah, I was called to speak to the world, although I was not totally aware of what He wanted me to do. Also, I just did not want to face what He called me to do. I still was afraid to speak out.

It was just a prayer, and while praying, God would guide me to pray for people. As I prayed, He would show me different ways to encourage them. As I grew closer to the Lord, He started to use me to share scriptures from the Bible with people as He led, but sometimes they were not well received because they may have revealed unreconciled sin in their life. My intentions were not to be nosey or judgemental, but only to be encouraging and obedient to the Lord. Many times they twisted scripture to justify their behavior. My father had a true saying, “Sometimes people make God in their own image.”

I took a word from Jesus very seriously, and I would have to account to Him one day. But I guess some things were too revealing, and they got mad. I had to obey what God told me, and if they had taken it in the right spirit in which it was presented, they would have been blessed. Instead of being so arrogant, they should have put their attitude at the foot of the Cross. God would have shown them what I was really saying; it was not to hurt but to help.

I learned much from my favorite book, *Rees Howells, Intercessor*. It revealed so much about how God worked in his life, and it encouraged me a lot. Rees Howells was a man peculiarly taught of God, one who learned the Bible as the Spirit made him live it. The book shows how he faced the implications of an entirely surrendered life, learned to love the unlovely, and found the key to prevailing prayer. He was taught the principles of divine healing and progressed ever further in faith until his prayers affected world events.

I would never tell anyone what God said unless He directed me to do so. I took His words seriously because they came from Jesus, and that was very important to me. I was there to encourage the hurting and wounded. If the people would have listened and been obedient, He would have blessed them greatly. I just gave the message and tried to pray them to victory; that was my job.

Many times, I felt helpless to help them, even though I knew that was not my job; it was the Holy Spirit's. I was to plant the seeds, and the Holy Spirit would do His work. God had given me the gift of love and a pure heart to cry out for all mankind.

Many people I did help, but some I didn't, and they turned on me. My heart broke because of the deep love I had for them all. I knew from my own life about being honest before Jesus, always keeping my attitude before the foot of the Cross, remaining humble with my heart in my hand, and giving it to Jesus. So, I would read the book of Jeremiah to help me understand my Heavenly Father more (Jeremiah 1).

My friends and I would get together and pray. We would seek God to know who and what to pray for. There were white witches in her neighborhood, and they knew we were there praying, so they wanted to meet me the next day and challenge me on God's word. I trusted Jesus to help me in this, and I went to meet them.

As I was traveling on a busy highway, I saw a huge crowd in the streets all around me. I was confused as to what was going on; was it a parade or something? I just sat at the light, watching what was there, and the light around me was very bright. I thought, *Wow, the sun is awful bright today.* All of a sudden, they were all gone. I knew then that God was showing me that He was sending His angels to be with me and keep me from harm. That was one of the first times I ever saw that angels were there to help us. I still remember it to this day and can see it in my mind. What peace came with their presence, not fear at all. Because these people wanted to hurt me and stop me from praying in their area where Satan had control, or so he thought (Hebrews 1:14).

My life and my children's lives were raised in the church, but the liars became very bad. The people were coming to my house and harassing me. Since I also taught the young adults class, some of the teenagers were out of control. They would tell their parents lies about me so they would not get into trouble if they misbehaved in church or were doing things they should not have been doing. I would never tell on them unless they were hurting themselves or others. But their parents would come to my house screaming at me; it hurt so bad because they would not listen to me. I just had to leave it in the hands of Jesus to straighten problems out. In the years that followed, these parents saw I was right.

My friends and I tried to defend me, but the elders would not listen. I loved them with all my heart, and it hurt a lot when they would not listen. Jesus told me to leave and go to another church, but I was so upset and lonely.

So many things were hitting me at once. They say one of the worst things in life is facing the death of a loved one and then a divorce. Well, it did not stop there. My love for this church, and my parents being upset with me, continued for five years. I was slipping backward, hurt from family, friends, and husbands. I was hurting so bad, I fell down in that hurt. People thought of the money I received from my husband's death and did not see the hurt and loneliness the kids and I felt. The money was there to support us until I could start working to support the family.

I wanted to dedicate my beauty shop to Jesus's glory, so I had my new Pastor come in and dedicate it to Jesus. I needed His wisdom and knowledge to go forward.

I could not believe I was opening a shop of my own. I did not think I could do it. I did my own books, supplies, advertising, and cleaning, plus I took care of the kids and house. Only Jesus could give me the wisdom and strength to do all these things.

As I opened my beauty shop, my girlfriend and my kids helped me do the repair work with my kids. Oh, we painted and laughed, we washed everything and laughed. A lot of hard work, but it was worth it for Jesus.

Satan was mad because we were there, and he sent people to bother us. Every day, one of the other store owners would curse me out for no apparent reason. He was not to be there, because I was supposed to be the only beauty shop in the shopping center. He got angry because I would not leave. One cold winter night at one a.m., he backed his red pickup truck through my front window which was three panes wide.

The police called me to come to the shop and have the windows boarded up so no one would get hurt. I had to take my two boys out of bed and take sleeping bags to the shop for them to sleep while I waited for a window repair man. It was so cold; we had no heat. The kids were tired and hungry and had to be up for school the next day.

The man who cursed me every day was warning me to leave. I was there for Jesus, and He will take care of us. And He did in every circumstance.

That other beauty shop had to close down; for what reason, I do not know.

Another time, a homeless woman who was not mentally well came into my shop and wanted her hair washed, so I did so. I was very uneasy with this, but I did not know how to turn her away. She would not leave, so I had to call the cops.

They said I should not have let her in because the night before, she injured a police officer and put him in the hospital. I was glad when she left peaceably. From then on, I had to keep my front door locked—not very business-like. I had to be careful because she would keep trying to come in until the police took her away.

I will never forget one particular event. I went to the beauty shop as usual. As I opened the door, I looked at the floor. I thought, *Wow, the floor was awfully shiny.* As I walked in, yes, it was very shiny, but it was not shine; it was water. The shop, from the back to the front, was flooded. What a clean-up job that was. Every day was a new event; I never knew what would happen in this shop.

There were a lot of good times. God blessed this shop with His presence all the time. Once, I was short on my rent, and a customer I had never seen before came in and said, "God said you are short on your rent. And I promised Him that if someone needs help, I will help, and He sent me to you. So here is a blank check. Fill in what you need, and I will sign it." I did not want to take the money; I was awestruck by it. But she insisted, so I did and paid my rent. Praise God.

I loved people and wanted to do my best to make them feel better about themselves and life. Getting their hair done lifts up people; just a kind word or a smile helps. Going the extra mile is seldom seen in this world today.

Hundreds of people walked through the doors of my shop as heathens and walked out knowing Jesus as their Savior, brand new creatures in Christ Jesus. I was familiar with hurt and pain, from death to divorce. Therefore, I could speak to others through firsthand experience of the awesomeness of God, that He forever reigns, saves, and keeps us continually. I believe the enemy was angry about my walk and the salvations that came out of my little shop because obstacles began to manifest almost immediately before we even opened the shop doors. One of the first obstacles that we encountered was the electricity. It was not turned on for three months. When I asked them why, there was no good reason for it; they didn't know why, either. What could I do?

Secondly, we had a fire that nearly destroyed us. It started a few stores down. The smoke traveled through all the ceilings and filled the shop with smoke. The smoke damaged the whole shop. I had to file an insurance claim, and they sent a cleaning crew to clean the shop. My friend and I had built this shop ourselves to save money, and with the setback of the fire, we found that we had to start all over again. These setbacks cost money, which I was running out of.

The shop had huge holes in the roof, and when it rained, the water would pour in. I would have to get out of bed at night and go to the shop to put out seven large pails to catch the water or face a flood. We also had mice and rats. One day, a customer was having her hair washed, leaning back in the sink, and saw the rats running in the ceiling lights. How was I going to explain this to a frightened customer? She seemed okay with it, then, but never came back.

I approached the landlord, and he did not want to hear anything. His answer was not a nice one, so I had to take care of it myself.

Oh, one more thing. A demon-filled young lady sat outside the shop for many days and would take off all her clothes. Yes, every word is true here. There were construction workers in the parking lot, and they egged her on, which upset me, so I called the police to stop this shameful event. It did not stop the power of God from working in that place, for the shop stood out like a light in a dark world.

As the business began to take off, I prayed for people who came in and needed help. I could help with money and food where it was needed. One time, a young girl whom I had never seen before came into the shop, and she told me she had just been saved. As she passed by, she felt led to come in and share something with me.

She told me that her father would molest her all the time, and she needed to tell someone that she forgave him. As she was speaking, I noticed the electrician that I had hired to repair some of the wiring in the shop was listening attentively to this young girl's story. I could see by his face that the story was touching his heart. I knew that God had a perfect plan in that encounter, and I thank Him for it.

Other times, when I was in the shop, people would come in and say, "Jesus sent me to pray with you." This always happened just at the times that I needed prayer and encouragement the most. He was making me into a stronger Christian woman each day. I am by nature quiet, mild, and sensitive, but through everything God has brought me through, He made me a strong, compassionate person, even though it was not easy for a self-employed woman on her own with four children.

Through these trials, Jesus used me to work with others and meet their needs so they may see Him. God taught me how to be strong yet sweet and loving, wise as a serpent yet gentle as a dove. He taught me how to yield myself to Him and live as a living sacrifice for His glory. I give Him all the praise, honor, and glory, for He is worthy.

One summer, God gave me and my children a great blessing. One of my friends took my two sons to her house in the country for the summer, which would free me up to take care of business at the shop without worrying about them. She and her husband took care of them as if they were their own children. Her husband took them under his wing and taught them things only a father could teach, and I was very thankful for that. They so missed a father's love. I did all I could do for them, but one thing I could not fulfill in their lives was a father's love. The boys had a great summer that year. They were getting older and needed a man's touch, and this man was ideal for them because he also loved Jesus and was a good example of a Christian man. To this day, my boys talk about those two summers and all the fun they had fishing and swimming in the creek at the back of their house.

One particular day, a strange thing happened. A wealthy, well-dressed woman in a full-length white mink coat pulled up in a limo and came into my beauty shop. She said that if I were to get rid of all these customers, she would come in with her wealthy friends. And they would make me a very rich person. As I listened to her, I felt like I was being tempted by Satan, who was trying to entice me to do wrong. Jesus spoke to my heart and said, "You will not be able to reach these people for me; they are like the young rich ruler who asked God, 'What must I do to be saved?' Jesus' reply was, 'Sell all you own and follow me. He said for this man it would be as if a camel could go through the eye of a needle'" (Matthew 19:16).

The shop was there for His glory right from the beginning, and Satan was angry and tried to stop me right from the start. Sure, it would have been good to have money supporting me and the children, but at what cost? My customers needed Jesus, and He knew their hearts and that they would come to Him.

My social security was running out, and I received no pay from the shop yet, so Satan tried to tempt me to take this lady's offer. But what would I profit if I gained the whole world and lost my soul? I was here to win souls for Jesus, not self-gain. I trusted in Jesus to take care of us.

He had a perfect plan for me. As my husband's social security benefits ran out, I had no way to support the house and the boys. My daughter was married then, so she moved back home and took over the house, and I turned it into a mother-and-daughter home. It worked out great, and to this day, we still live together, but this time, I live with her. Praise God, we are together. What a blessing to see my grandchildren grow up. He supplied my needs once again. Nothing is impossible with God if we just put our trust in Him.

The lady who owned the shop before me wanted to sell it for twenty thousand dollars, and I went to the shop and prayed. God showed me that there was something going on behind the scenes. As I did this, I felt in my spirit something was wrong. When we went into closing on this business, my lawyer looked over their papers and said to me not to buy this shop. He saw that there was no money that came in for months, and all the workers left the shop to work somewhere else.

I was not aware of this at the time. It was a poor business deal, and it hurt because I knew the people I was buying from and trusted them. They were Christians, and I did not think they would have done that. I just knew that God wanted me there.

I walked away from that shop but did not forget it. A while went by, and I went back to look at the shop; it was closed. So, I went to the landlord and asked to rent this shop; it was already set up as a beauty shop. I knew this was the place for me. The previous owners had a bad reputation, so I had to build the shop up from the bottom. I was upset with them because they were selling me nothing, no goodwill at all. I worked long, hard hours to the point of a complete loss of strength.

Everyone knows themselves the best, and what I am today is what God made through me in spite of myself. I know my weaknesses and strengths. I was put down a lot in life and had no self-confidence because of it; it stopped me from going forward many times. I was afraid to talk and express myself in many ways. Instead of speaking when something wrong was done, I would just walk away upset. It made it difficult to develop in later years, and many times, I stayed in pain.

I was growing daily through His word and prayer; they strengthened me so much. I loved to pray, so I would pray for whoever God put before me. My friends and I would go to different homes and pray for people, bringing hope and peace to many individuals. What joy to be used by God as His instrument of love to this world!

Events occurred during my life's journey as I was working, and it was hard to leave my children at home alone. Yes, they were in their teens, but I believed to be there for them. One of my sons was fooling around with one of his friends, wrestling on the lawn. One of the neighbor men saw them, thought they were really fighting, and punched my son in the stomach, knocking the wind out of him. In times like this, I missed my husband handling this matter, and the children missed him, too. But he wanted nothing to do with them, not even his son. He told me before he left that he hated them and never wanted to see them again, and he never did. I was so upset that a person could say such a thing; he was their dad now, and he adopted them.

I never shared much of what was going on within my family. I did not want our parents distressed like I was. It was six long years of his cruel behavior, knowing when he walked through that door, he would be angry and take it out on us. I felt like I was back at home with my mom, who acted the same way. Always fighting with everyone, never a smile on their face. Picking on everything in life and making everyone around them wish he could be happy.

God had to show me that it was not up to me to make him happy; that was his responsibility. Because I tried everything I could to help him. I saw what was happening to him; he was backsliding into the world, listening to people outside our home. At work, the women flirted with him, and the men made fun of him because he married a widow with three children.

What could I do but trust Jesus to take care of him? Because I was running out of strength. He was getting out of hand, drinking and coming home drunk in front of the children, having a girlfriend, coming home smelling like perfume, buying her presents, leaving where I could find them, and not giving me any money for the household. I did not understand how he could be so cruel. We had a son together; what about him? I thought that not even some animals would act this way.

I was very determined to make this marriage work. I knew it was of God, so I just walked in faith, doing whatever Jesus showed me to do to be the best Christian wife I could be.

It was as if my husband was mentally torturing me, and Jesus wanted it to stop. It was hard for me to believe this dream because I was under the impression that God would not make bad things happen. I learned through the years that this is not true. He would keep us through problems in life. As much as God tried to show my husband he was on the wrong road, he would not listen. Satan wanted to destroy the marriage and hurt many people around us in the process. We are not an island unto ourselves.

His parents said, "Why did you not share this

with us?" I loved them so much that it hurt too much to talk about it with anyone. And my parents had been through enough with me; how could I tell them?

I know this upset my son just as much as me; he loved his stepdad. At times, I grew weary, and much prayer was needed, so on my knees I went once again, crying out to God with my hurts.

As I was in prayer, God showed me Jesus on a donkey and people waving palms before Him (Zechariah 9:9, KJV). Then, I knew victory was ahead in life. I worried much about the children because I knew they were hurting as well. They needed a dad who loved them, for at times, they would share a hurt, which brought tears to my eyes. I wanted them to learn forgiveness, which is a hard lesson to learn when you are suffering so badly and are as young as they were. But Jesus gave me a verse: "And be ye kind one to another, tenderhearted, forgiving one another, even as God for Christ's sake hath forgiven you (Ephesians 4:32, KJV).

Did I make the right decisions in life? I questioned my decision to remarry. Even though it was too late to change things, I still questioned myself. Then God showed me a scripture verse on this matter. "And Abraham said unto his eldest servant of his house ... he shall send his angel before thee, and thou shalt take a wife unto my son from thence" (Genesis 24:2,7, KJV). And I rested in His wisdom what was best for us all.

Jesus has given me many encouraging words throughout my life; they came from people in the Bible, or a sermon. And when they came, they just warmed my heart, and I knew, once again, He reached down and touched my life like only He could do.

8
Family

God's word was real and alive to my children and me, who, through all the turmoil, were cheerful and fairly well-adjusted after all they had been through. God held us tightly together, making us a very close, strong family. Even to this day, as my children have married and have children of their own, we remain a very strong family unit. I have four children, seven grandchildren, and two step-grandchildren whom I love very much. I am so happy and proud of them all.

Many miraculous events occurred in my life, and there were several instances, especially as I was going through these hard times, when I knew my Heavenly Father was right beside me. At one point, I desperately needed a new car, so I brought the need to the Lord, and every morning, I took my Bible and my praise music, went to my favorite beach, and began to pray. One day, as I was praying, the Holy Spirit directed me to a car dealership, and I asked God, "Is this really You,

Lord?" I had no money or credit, and I knew that buying a new car was impossible in natural circumstances. I had kept trying to fix and repair my old car, which was irreparable. But I kept trying to fix the old car, and the repair man said he could not fix it; the bill came to 5,000 already. I realized the Lord was speaking to me when the car could not be repaired. So, I stepped out in faith and went to a dealership.

Jesus showed me which dealership to go to, and I just obeyed His lead. I did not know the people there, but Jesus said to go there, so I went. It seemed like a nice place, and I felt the Lord leading me there.

I filled out the loan application and handed it to the loan officer. I thought to myself, *What am I doing? No money, no co-signer, nothing but faith.* I almost chickened out and ran.

The loan agent took one look at my completed application, laughed at me, and threw the pages back in my face. But I kept continuously praying, and I said, "Lord, I know You sent me here; I came here in faith." Unbeknownst to me, as the loan agent was throwing the pages at me, the owner of the store came in and saw what the agent had done. The owner came up to me and asked If I was my youngest son's mom. I said, "Yes, how do you know me?" He explained that he knew my son and told me to go outside and pick out whichever vehicle I wanted and not to worry about the credit issue; he would give me all the credit I needed.

There are three interesting things related to this story. First, the day I went to the dealership, my son was unaware that I was there or that I was even looking for a car at that time. Secondly, the loan agent, who threw the application back at me, was terminated from his employment at the dealership. Thirdly, my son-in-law is still driving that car today, plus I did not know my son knew this dealership. I just stepped out in faith, trusting Jesus to take care of us. He knew I needed a good car so I could take care of all of us. What a great car it was; it lasted forever.

Even though we had many hard times, Jesus always took care of us. I always paid my bills on time, we had plenty of food, and we lived in a beautiful house in a good neighborhood with good schools. Jesus was true to His word: the righteous shall not be forsaken nor their seed begging for bread (Psalm 37:25, KJV). He says in His word, “But seek ye first the kingdom of God, and his righteousness; and all these things shall be added unto you” (Matthew 6:33). I found Him to be true to every word in the Bible; I lived it.

At times, it produced jealousy in people around

me. My chief desire was to be a peacemaker, and after all the tragedy I experienced, I needed people to love me because I felt so unloved. But it seemed that all they saw was the material things, a nice house in a good neighborhood, and a good car.

I only had these items because Jesus gave them to me. Whatever money I had, I used for God's glory by opening up the beauty shop, from which I never took a salary. I had many hard times with not having money; it was not easy raising four children alone. I never told anyone. I just went to Jesus with my problems.

They never saw my hurt and pain, but Jesus did and was my constant guide and comfort. Though I might not have had millions of dollars, I had all my beautiful children, which left me rich beyond anything on this earth.

As the children got older, they married and went off on their own, and I got lonely. But Jesus filled my life with Him.

He sent me such great friends. One couple has taken me into their home many times and shared their home with me to stay with them for weeks at a time. Their whole family treated me very special. Their kindness strengthened my heart. Their home was beautiful, way out in the country. I would go for walks and pray as I read my Bible, getting closer to God daily. They had a room for me, put a television for me in it, and fixed it so pretty. I was so touched by their generosity and kindness. My children loved them when they saw how kind they were to me. We became friends from me cutting their hair for many years, and we stayed friends. I love them so much and thank God for their lives; they gave me confidence in life once more. It is not just going to church to know Jesus but having Him as your best friend; He became so real to me, and my friends watched Jesus live through me.

My Bible was my constant companion and guide, Jesus my shield and buckler. I have never been moved from my walk in Him, and he raised me up from the dead in my flesh and planted my feet on a highway of faith. There was no doubt in my heart and mind that Jesus was real. Only Jesus could have made me into a new person made in His image. Each day, my flesh died and was then made over in His image so He could live through me, so I could share His great love with others. I found myself meek, mild, and strong in the flesh, and through His precious Holy Spirit, I became one with Jesus.

It was not always an easy road, but when He saved me, He said I was to follow Him along the road He chose for my life. And I did not know what He was talking about, but I learned to trust Him, for He knew what was best for me. Sometimes I learned that the hard way when I would do my own thing. His Word says to try the spirits and make sure they are of Him. *So I tried.*

I had to learn spiritual warfare, to rebuke Satan when he would come and try to tell me that I was no good and that the children and I would be unable to survive. It was important not to listen to his lies. I always knew the self-deprecating thoughts that would creep into my mind were not true, but I still had to overcome this battle and, occasionally, still deal with it to this day. Being told all my life not to do this and that was a hard thing to overcome. I knew I was always meek; through Jesus, I was not weak. Even though we cannot see the end, Jesus can and knows what is best for us. If we give in to Satan, we will lose the blessing that is ahead.

9
Protection

One day, my legs were hurting so bad. I did not have enough money to go to a doctor. I heard of a new clinic that opened not far from my house, so I went. They checked my legs and sent me to a hospital to be checked. As the doctor was checking my legs, he got a little out of place, putting his hands where they did not belong. There was a resident physician in the back room, and when he heard me telling the doctor to stop touching me, the resident yelled at him. The doctor finally backed away from me and left me alone. He then wrote a prescription for me, and I took it for a month.When I returned for a check-up, there was a new woman doctor who re-checked me and said, "Who gave you this medication?" I said, "The last doctor who checked me." She was very angry with him and told me not to take these pills; they were very bad for me. They will make you gain about 40 pounds, and you will never be able to lose that weight because it will lock into your body cells.

I was so upset because I have always had a weight problem. Now what? In the following months, I started to gain weight for no good reason. I was so upset and did not know what to do, so I dieted very hard. Yet, the weight would not come off. That lady doctor was right about that medication. So, I just trusted Jesus on this, and as the years passed, I started to lose weight, but it was very hard, and it took me about 15 years to see some results. But Jesus did protect me from a crazy doctor.

If you are ever to be strong in Jesus and in the power of His might, your strength will be born during a storm (Eph. 6:10).

I knew in my spirit that the only truth was that my Heavenly Father would take care of His children and that He would never leave or forsake us because He loved us. One day, Jesus led me to pray around my house for protection. We were alone, the children and I, and we needed Jesus to take care of us like a husband and father would. Well, I walked around the house and prayed. I knew there was a dark spirit outside the house trying to enter to disrupt our home. Jesus opened my spiritual eyes, and I saw it running around frantically, trying to get in. You know how Satan is; he tried to put doubt in my mind that what I saw did not really happen.

I had company that week, and we were sitting at my kitchen table by the window. My visitor said, "What is that thing running around the house, a black dog? We kept looking outside at it because it was getting annoying. She was a young believer, and it touched me that she saw it as well. We watched it and saw it was not a dog. I told her that Satan was trying to enter this house in one form or another so he could only do his dirty work through a body, human or animal, but he could not enter, for I prayed and sealed my house with the blood of Christ. Satan could not hurt us now.

As the years passed, I grew more and more as a Christian. I saw God's hand protecting us. We had a bad hurricane one year, and I lived close to the bay. They were evacuating the houses in my area, and my dad called to tell me to get out now before it was too late to leave. As he was speaking to me on the telephone, it went dead. I prayed so hard on what I should do and felt in my spirit that we would be OK. The other people on our block went to the school for shelter until the storm passed.

As I was standing by my kitchen window watching the storm, a still small voice said, "Pray now against the wind for God to hold it back." Before I did that, I heard a loud wind around the house, but when I spoke those words, the wind stopped. The wind hit my house, but only a storm window broke. The regular window behind it was just fine. No water was able to come into the house.

The lights and heat were out for two weeks, and food was low. One of my nephews came one day with a cooler full of food for us. God had to touch his heart to help me, for I had no money or food, and we were in a dark, cold house. The children slept by the fireplace, which kept us warm and gave us light at night. The trees were down around us, and there was no way out of our block, so we could not go for help. The peace of Jesus was with us; we made it like a campout. We were all safe; that is what mattered most. You can replace material things; they rust and decay sooner or later. Trusting in God this way brought a deeper faith into our lives.

Wow, another miracle from His tender love once more. How can I not tell of His precious love, not just for Him saving me, but for taking care of us all?

I found that some of the people who surrounded me during those times, both my family and Christian friends, were much like Job's friends. I had to separate myself from everyone who spoke against the Word I was standing on, lean on Jesus, and know that he loved me and was guiding me all the way.

This time in my life is comparable to when Jesus told Paul in the Bible the things he would suffer for the gospel's sake; my heart's desire was for my family and me to serve the Lord and glorify Him. If that meant taking a stand for Christ, regardless of the obstacle or hindrance, then so be it. There were occasions after I made this decision that the children didn't like it very much. I stood my ground, for the Bible speaks of the priest who did not discipline his children and was put to death. I wanted a life of godliness for my children, for I knew they needed to know boundaries to have a solid foundation.

They were good children but needed guidance like us all. Once, they said, "We are good kids; you should see what other kids are into." I told them they are not who we should compare ourselves to. We should try to please Jesus, not the world.

When I was first born again, I was slain in the Spirit, and Jesus showed me many things that were to come and about His return. As the head of the household, I knew that I was responsible for the welfare and spiritual growth of my four children. I understood that this kind of life would be hard on them. They had to find Jesus for themselves; that would be the only way they could make it in Jesus. Not because I was saved; they had to ask Him in their own hearts. I knew that a person on fire for God could make it through;

this revelation kept me on course. I wanted my children's lives, as well as my own, to glorify God at any cost. I dedicated our lives to Him, and as He led us through life, we would learn to walk on water (by faith) by His loving grace.

I know I had to be honest and fair with the children. I never wanted to lie or be a phony to them. What is wrong is wrong, and we must own up to it, no matter what it may be. I just wanted to be an honest person before the Lord. It hurt me when I had to stand my ground, but I knew if I did not, Jesus would not be pleased with me as a parent. I know they did not understand me at times, but I prayed that Jesus would show them someday that I did this out of love.

I was very young when I got married, so I believe I grew up with my children. My mom was 15 when she married my dad, and back then, it was fine. I was 17 years old and still a baby, and my husband was 21. We learned to be good parents as we went along, trying to do what was right. I know we did the best we could, and what we did wrong, I hope my children can forgive me one day because I love them so much and lived for them, not myself.

I would never want to hurt them or anyone else.

10

Loving People

I wanted to go to Bible school, but I found this impossible with four children under my wing. One time in prayer, the Holy Spirit spoke to me and said He would teach me through His Word, and teach me He did. I watched miracle after miracle happen. When we were sick, He healed us; when we were hungry, He fed us to the point that one day, food was left on my doorstep by someone we didn't know. No one knew our circumstances, that there was no food in the house at that time.

One time, my youngest son was very sick with a high fever and went into convulsions; his eyes rolled to the back of his head, and then he collapsed, which I had never seen before. I did not know what to do. I immediately called on the name of Jesus to help him, and my son opened his eyes and sat up straight, looking at me, smiling as if nothing had happened; his fever broke, and he was completely healed.

These are just some of the miracles that happened during trying times in our lives. God became the husband and father to the children and me; He would do the same for anyone who asks. When I was lonely, He was with me; I was not alone. When I mourned, He comforted me. He has blessed me tremendously, from Godly parents to grandparents, all the way to my children and grandchildren.

At this point, my story is just beginning, and through this next life experience, I learned again that no weapon formed against me would prosper (Isaiah 54:17).

The church that I was attending became such a hindrance to the children and me. This was my family's church and the one in which I was saved, but I had entered a season where it seemed I could do nothing right. My children watched hurtful events unfold, but it was a good experience for them to learn forgiveness. The children saw me daily, so they knew my behavior in church was the same as it was out of church, that I lived a true sincere walk with Jesus. I just did not read the Bible; I lived it the best I could.

I was holding prayer meetings at church on Wednesday mornings, and many people attended. Jesus blessed us with many victories in our lives. Plus, we were so blessed with His presence to heal and deliver people from depression and sicknesses. One time, my friend, as she was praying, had a vision of someone stabbing me in the back. As time went on, we understood what this vision meant: people were talking against me, and God was warning us what was happening. I just continued to go on and trust Him to take care of this matter. I just wanted to Glorify Him. Behind the scenes, Satan was stirring up trouble to try to stop God's work. God showed me that when my work was done, He would move me on, but I did not understand that at that time. I just put my trust in Him, for I wanted to please and work for Him; I love Him so.

I love to work for Jesus, and I wanted to tell the world of His great love and mercy. If we turn our lives to Him, He will have all the answers in His Word. Pray first and read His Word; He will guide you throughout your life. Jesus never failed me, even when I did not understand His will, but hindsight and trusting Him brought me through many times.

The children did not come with an instruction book, and many times, I did not know what to do. But Jesus knows each heart, and He directed me on how to meet each of their needs. Each child is different, and how you deal with one does not always work for another. I love my children very much, and I humbled myself before the Cross so

I may become a better mother. Not just a better mother but a friend, sister, aunt, wife, daughter, and servant before the Lord. I know we are not perfect; we can never be, only Jesus is, but I tried my best.

I am not here to please the world, only Jesus. He died for us, and I wanted to live for Him. I knew I had a lot to learn from Him in order to grow in His Word; that is why I prayed and studied so constantly. I love the Word; it gives me peace, strength, and rest to overcome the world and its temptations and not to take the wrong road in life. This is so important because Satan is always there trying to lead us away from our walk in Christ Jesus.

I had gotten a little discouraged with what was going on in the church. I did not understand what was going on around me, knowing I was staying close to Jesus. I thought we were all on the same side.

My church continued to have issues with me. Then the Lord spoke to me in prayer to be still and know that He is God. My chief issue was that two of my "friends," who were both in sin, went to the elders to complain about me. The elders listened to them. At that time, the elders were not aware of what they were doing, and Jesus told me not to tell because one was a babe in Christ. If the elders knew, it would be very hard on them, and they would lose their salvation. I did not want to have that on me. In time, He would deal with them.

I promised Jesus that I would not defend myself as He told me; He will exalt me in due season. He did deal with it; He sent two friends to expose the lies about me, confirming that I was not saying and doing wrong things against His Word. Jesus even sent others to speak for me. They still would not listen. I felt so not wanted. Jesus said leave now. It was so hard to leave my home church where I got saved; I loved them so much.

My time did come, as many people tried to rescue and defend me. They said, "If she leaves this church, the Holy Spirit will also leave." No one would listen to this, and I was not aware of what was going on. People started to leave the church, and even the elders' own close families left. The church was almost empty, and after a while, there were very few services to this very day; so sad.

God was trying to bring truth to the church, but no one wanted to listen. Too much pride in their lives. I took my children and went to another church where God used my son with another Christian boy who wanted to commit suicide. I praised God that we listened and went there, allowing us to save this teenager's life.

One of the mistakes I had made in church, which caused me considerable difficulty, was that I put the elders before Jesus. I listened to their words before I listened to what God said in His Word. The elders would tell me if I did not obey what they were telling me, they would not counsel me anymore. I knew in my spirit that they were wrong; what I was being told did not line up with the Word.

Time and time again, they became very angry with me, saying things from the pulpit. During this one time, they were speaking against me, and Jesus sent someone over to me and said not to listen; it was not of God. I was hurting so bad. As I prayed, God showed me they were wrong. With love, I tried to explain what was going on, but they would not listen. Then, they just stopped talking to me altogether. I came to realize that we are all human, and I must forgive my pastor and forget about the hurt that I had received from the elders' words. I was aware of the Scripture, which clearly states, "Touch not God's anointed and do no harm" (Psalm 105:15), so I left this matter in Jesus' hands. He is on the Throne, and it is up to Him to take care of this. I really was not too clear on what was happening.

Many church members told them if I left the church, it would be considered Ichabod, meaning the Holy Spirit left the church. All I ever wanted to do was pray because my gift is to be a prayer warrior.

I loved the people in my church very much; they are great people and have done a lot of good. We all make mistakes in life. I was not aware of anything that happened after I left, but as years passed, things came to my attention.

Many people were saved through my walk with Jesus; a few examples are listed below. My first husband's father did not believe in God at all, but when he had gotten along in years, he became very ill and was sent to the hospital. He began to call out to God. Interestingly, I had a prompting in my spirit to pray for him as well, as he was very sick. I was not aware that he was in the hospital at all.

Although we were not close, I knew he needed Jesus, and I prayed for him very hard. He felt the only way he could get to see me and my children and make things right between us was by praying so I would go visit him in the hospital. He knew that the children and I had a relationship with Jesus. As he was praying, God led me to see Dad in the hospital, and I did not even know he was there until he contacted me. Dad said that he prayed, and Jesus appeared to him, and he asked Jesus to forgive him of his sins. Then he asked his wife and me for forgiveness as well. He said he should have been a better husband, father-in-law, and grandfather. He said when he gets well, he will do better, which he never did. He went home to Jesus. I consider it to have been a privilege to lead him to the Lord, for I loved him so.

My father-in-law had always been unkind to me, and I never knew why. When I visited him, he kissed and hugged me for the first time since I met him. What miracles God does in our lives! God has forgiveness for us all, and we are to forgive as well. What freedom we receive from His tender mercy.

There were times that I became discouraged, especially after the conflict with my church. Although I loved my church, Jesus said it was time for me to move on. I was obedient and did so, but I missed everyone and all the events that I was involved in. I had spent many hours there working on whatever needed to be done, from cleaning to teaching a class. Some people were for me, and some were against me, and they let me know it.

But it was time to move out of my comfort zone and onto another level in my walk. It was not an easy change for me because the people in my old church were my lifeline at that time. I went to another church, but my heart was broken from the many hurts and disappointments over the years.

I was growing weary. It was getting hard to trust people since I was really close to one of them. She turned against me and said many hurtful lies. I had to realize that she was messed up and hurting within herself.

I spent much time in the Word, and I knew that I was more than a conqueror through Jesus Christ. During these down times, the Lord would show me that my victory was and is complete in Him. I was not defeated or destroyed. He would deal with the situation, and I thanked God for the battle, even though, at times, it was so hard for me to let go and let God be God. Many times, I had to reminisce and see where he brought me from to where I am now, which gave me great encouragement. I loved Christian music, which filled my heart with victory and great peace.

Time and time again, I would see God's hand move on my behalf. During these times, I learned about spiritual warfare by myself. Looking into God's Word and as I learned, the teachings became so real to my children and me. Satan is real, and he destroys lives by lying and deceiving. We would fight through the battles together through prayer and leave to rest to Him. He says the battle is His, not ours.

11

Scared

One day, on my way home from church, I was alone, and I stopped to have pizza for lunch. I had gone to that pizza place for eighteen years, so I felt safe there. Well, as I entered, I was not aware it was not open yet. The owner said, "Hi, come in. We are not open yet, but I have made some chicken. Would you like to have some with me?" I said no thank you, but he would not take no for an answer.

He said to come to a back table and have some chicken. It seemed harmless enough. I trusted him because I had been going to this pizza place for a long time, and he was married with children who worked there with him. I did not think anyone could be so bold. He started to make a pass at me and asked me personal questions. He asked me to date him, even though he was married. I knew I was in some kind of trouble at this point, and fear started to come over me. I started to call on Jesus for help, asking what I should do at that moment.

He talked about watching me as I shopped around town in such a weird way I became frightened. He said he wanted to be with me, and he grabbed me. He was getting angry and started to talk about raping me now or being his girlfriend so he could have me all the time.

I was so afraid I did not know what to do, so I started praying, "My heavenly Father, please help me; this man is going to hurt me." All of a sudden, he pulled away, and I said to him, "Let me think about it. I will let you know." As I walked to the door, he unlocked it. I did not know he had locked me in, and it was a good thing because I would have been more afraid. Well, I got out of there fast, my body frightfully shaking.

For a year, I had nightmares about this pizza man and was afraid to go out. A male member of my family went and had a talk with him, which ended it all. I did not want to tell the kids; I did not want them to worry about me. As a parent, you always want to protect them from this world.

Once again, I thank God for saving my life. He was my Savior and King, the omnipotent God, knowing all and seeing all. I was learning through these times to have dancing faith like Haggai 2:19: "Is the seed yet in the barn? Yea, as yet the vine, and the fig tree, and the pomegranate, and the olive tree, hath not brought forth; from this day will I bless you."

As I studied this scripture verse, I realized this was a dancing faith Haggai had. The lesson here is that even if there is nothing left, do not look at your surroundings. Just keep your mind and heart before God.

God is good, and no good thing will He withhold from me. He is always with us wherever we go and takes care of us. I believe there have been many times He has protected us from harm that we were unaware of. Thank you, Jesus, for your loving care.

As the years passed, the children were going toward adulthood, and I was fighting diligently for them by caring for them. I failed to fight for myself. I still had moments when I felt that I was not worth fighting for, and I actually allowed the enemy's lies regarding my unworthiness to affect me for many years. I should have been proud of how God worked through me. I was very proud of the children, but I failed to give myself any "pats on the back," yet I was the person all alone raising them. I also forgot to take care of my body, and I did not eat right, sleep, or exercise. I wore my body down. I made sure *they* ate right, slept well, and did well in school. I just wanted to take good care of them and did not want them to feel that because they had no dad, we were not a whole family. Sometimes, I was so tired I fell asleep at the kitchen table.

There was an unsaved member of our family who was very set in her ways. She seemed to me a very hardcore person and would never let anyone close to her. She said to me one day, "I never had a friend." She was not my type of friend because she argued with everyone and wanted to fistfight. That was not the kind of person I wanted to be around. But Jesus knew her heart was hurting and wanted me to be there for her. We became close, and she would email me so we could talk.

She came over for a visit one day, and I asked her if she would like to go to church with me, and she said yes. We went, and it was a good service that day, with the pastor speaking on salvation. The pastor asked if there was anyone there that day who wanted to give their heart to Jesus. He also said this may be your last chance. She turned to me and said, "That is for me, but I will not do it."

After church, we went for a ride and lunch; no more was said about the sermon. She liked to read, and I gave her a book called "Rees Howells, Intercessor" by Norman Grubb; this man loved the Lord. Weeks went by, and we shared emails in which she said she loved the book and learned so much from it. She knew then that she was wrong about her beliefs. Jesus worked with her on her own ground and touched her heart, which was the best healing anyone could receive. She gave her heart to Jesus and was such a different person; it was so hard to believe. Just think, if I had kept my bad attitude about her, she might never have gotten saved and been in heaven now. This taught me a good lesson about myself.

Within the weeks that followed, she came down with lung cancer, and we were all distressed to see her so sick. We prayed for a healing, but Jesus took her home to be with Him. Since her heart belonged to Jesus, what better place could she be, with no more pain, just pure joy? Even though we may miss her, she is in a better place; no more sickness. Praise God.

She said to me, "Jesus had to take me this way because I was too stubborn to listen to Him the first time." I was passing a store, and a beautiful pink angel stood there. I wanted to buy it for her, but I did not have money, only a maxed-out credit card. I tried anyway and bought her that angel, which she kept by her bed and wanted to be buried with.

How Jesus knows every heart. Her family was not happy, for they were of a different religion, and they told her not to listen. But she found Jesus and was so in love with Him that it did not matter to her that she was so ill. She knew that soon she would see Jesus face-to-face, and she had a great peace that passed all human understanding. What a wonderful God we serve; His mercy endures forever.

Through this, all members of her family gave their hearts to Jesus. What a mighty God we serve!

My middle son always wanted to fly a plane, so he entered college to fly. He completed a year and received his pilot's license for small aircraft.

As he sought God to determine what direction to take in life, he got his answer: join the Marines Corp. As you would guess, that would not have been my first choice for him, being a mother.

God had already prepared my heart for this request by showing me that he was going to join the Marines. I was in bed that night, and my son came home from work, knelt by my bed, and said, "Mom, God wants me to go into the Marines Corp." My heart sank because I knew what a tough outfit they were; his dad was a Marine.

He never met his dad because he died before he was born, but little does he know he looks just like him. I knew in my heart he was to go, and I would miss him a lot; all of us here would miss him. His younger brother had slept in the same room with him since they were babies, and when his brother left to go into the Marine Corps, he would now sleep in that room, missing him so much. Once, I found him sleeping on the couch in the living room. We had a sad household for a while. But we were very proud of him in the Marines; he did a great job there, and his drill instructor liked him very much.

I knew God had His hand on my son and a calling that only my son could do. Since he was four years old, he loved Jesus and His Word. While he was in the Marines, God used him to save a backslidden young Christian Marine. He was only 18 years old and could not take the pressure of the Corp. My son would watch him because he did not seem okay.

One late evening, my son looked up from his bunk, and this backslidden young Christian boy had hung himself by their bunk. My son cut him down right away and saved his life. Through prayer, he returned him to Christ's side again. He sat with him all night so there would be no more trouble. Then, the next day, he told the drill instructor what happened. They contacted the boy's parents right away, and he was discharged from the Marines. His parents were so thankful that my son saved their son's life.

God used my son many times there with his fellow Marines. While he was there, he got married to a great Christian girl. They opened their home to many lonely and homesick Marines, feeding and caring for them as if they were his family.

My older son worked on Wall Street with many self-made men who felt they did not need God, yet Jesus used him in this hardcore world with great honors. I had prayed continuously to have bright children who would pray and witness to the unsaved world and pull them out of the fires of hell.

My older son did not come to Jesus at an early age. He was the kind of man who had to find out things for himself. Jesus had told me that one day, he would be saved. Many nights, I did not get off my knees praying for him.

I would pray, "Lord, you know where he is and what he is doing. Send your Holy Spirit to touch his heart." A few years went by, and he went to college. The college offered a Bible course, and he took it. As he listened to his professor explain the Bible, he would go back to our church and ask questions of our assistant pastor, who was a professor at the same college. God touched my son's heart, and he gave it willingly over to Jesus and became a true Christian. I was so amazed to see the change in him. God was true to His word. He spoke to me about him, and I would not pressure him about getting saved. I just trusted Jesus because this son was very strong-willed, and only Jesus could deal with him.

God directed him to a Spanish church, even though we are Italian Americans. He felt that was where God called him to be. He studied Spanish, and he loved it. He does much work for the Lord and travels all over, speaking and helping others. He has a precious heart for Jesus, and the more we talk together, the more I see how he is growing in the Lord. You do not know how proud I am of that. I obeyed God and backed off him, allowing him to find his own way. I am very proud that he turned out to become a man after God's own heart.

My daughter worked with me in the beauty shop as a hairdresser and married a Christian man. My youngest son was a great blessing; he continually touches the world around him with his tender spirit. He loves to help people in whatever way he can, no matter who they may be: his neighborhood, family, friends, or a stranger stuck on the side of the road. As I contemplate the beautiful lives of my four children, I see God's love for me. *What more could a mother want?* I ask myself.

Through these up and down periods in my life, I realized why reading the Word of God was so important. The Word tells us not to grow weary in well-doing, for we will reap what we sow if we faint not (Galatians 6:9). His Word strengthens and guides us on our road in life and gives us much peace as we go.

I was fighting discouragement, which will affect your whole life. Like me, you lose your confidence and develop a negative spirit. You talk yourself into a mess in life, and you think you are right in your thoughts. I looked around me and saw other people being happy, prosperous, and, of course, with husbands. God showed me one thing about looking at others: that all that glitters is not gold. The grass is not always greener somewhere else. My dad had a saying: "It is a great life if you do not weaken." How true!

I was envious of my neighbor, who had a husband, and wished it was me. Then I found out that he left her, and she was miserable and was drinking. Well, I learned that I did not have it so bad.

I was running from life and did not want to face life because I had no confidence in myself anymore. I thought I needed a husband to make it in life. And if my husbands did not love me, I must be unlovable. So, I closed my heart to everyone. Satan planted the doubts, and I ran with them. He said, "Where is God now?" I was in such pain that I started to listen to Satan's lies, which were to destroy God's word within me.

I loved the Lord but was afraid to put my trust in Him because of what happened in my past. Satan would whisper, "If He really loved you, then what is going on?" But I learned now that if I had just trusted Him and His word, it would have been much easier for me, for Jesus would have broken the chains of doubt right away. I know now it was a school of learning for me. Hindsight was a great teacher for me back then. I was younger, still growing in Jesus, and would get weary and discouraged. It was like I walked into a different world; it was a nightmare, and I could not get a grip on life, and I fell down. I did not leave the Lord—just kind of sunk in misery, which is a bad place to be, for Satan can torment you there with lies.

We must stay in His love so we can be reachable. I just lay like a lump and did not fight back at Satan's lies. Now, I know that standing on Jesus's promises would have given me victory much sooner instead of being Satan's punching bag. In hindsight, it was a learning experience I will not forget, for when Satan attacks me now, I fight back.

I was tired working so hard, scared, lonely, and had no confidence in myself, not realizing I am what God made of me. I was not trusting God, how He made me was greater than I realized. All our life experiences are there only as stepping stones. They prepare us for a future in Christ and His work so we may become stronger, wiser, and walk on His solid road of love.

I was afraid to go ahead in life because of my past. I thought, "Oh, no, what's coming ahead is more pain," so I froze. As I looked back while writing this book, I learned so much about myself and how GREAT my God is, which makes me stronger for future events. I do not fall down so easily now, not without a fight, with Jesus on my side. I thank Him for being patient with me and knowing my heart. I was not being rebellious; I was confused and did not know what was happening. As I am writing this now, I cry, having to remember the hurts of the past and the old me. But I am going through every day and learning to trust Jesus.

Going back to when I was saved and Jesus spoke to my heart, He said, "When you give your life to me, you must walk the road I have chosen for you." I can still hear His voice echo in my mind as clear as a bell. My experience helped get me through.

I am so grateful that He never gave up on me and was with me every moment. Even when I failed Him, He forgave me. I know now my life went according to His plan. I should have done better, but He understood me better than I understood myself. God will not give up on us; just don't quit. If we don't quit, He will not quit. Amen!

It takes courage to be obedient to Him, which only He can give if you put your trust in Him.

I did grow weary at times with myself because I was trying to live by the law of the Word alone and not allowing room for the Holy Spirit to work together with me, as Paul writes in Romans 7:17-25.

There was so much to learn, but the Holy Spirit was patient with me and taught me much. I had to learn to be patient with myself. When I erred, I was very hard on myself and would not let it go. I learned from King David how he sinned with Bathsheba and murdered her husband, and eventually was forgiven by God (2 Samuel 11).

I thought once you were saved, you did not sin anymore, which is totally wrong. We will sin, but with a sincerely repented heart before the Lord, we do not do it again. We go to our Heavenly Father and ask Him to help us, to give us the strength to walk in Him. God knows our hearts, but it is not a license to sin. I learned God forgives us, for we all sin and fall short of His Glory; only He was perfect. One sin is as bad as another. There is no big sin or little ones; sin is sin. God sent the prophet Nathan to David and exposed his sin. David heard what the prophet said and repented. Jesus at Calvary died for our sins. He covered all of them even though we were yet in sin. What great love He has for us! He paid the price not just for our sins but for our healing. He paid the price for the whole world (1 Corinthians 15; John 3:3-21).

So, if you do not know Jesus, invite Him into your heart today. You will never regret it. Take it from me; I am much older today and have never stopped loving Him, and He never stopped loving me.

My love for the Word and for Jesus kept me on the right road, and His love for me carried me throughout life's journey.

There is a song I love to listen to, and it fits me: "It's my Desire."

It's my desire to live for Jesus,
It's my desire to live for Him;
Though often failed Him,
And caused Him shame.
It's my desire to live for Him.

If we come to Him in our failing life and repent, Jesus will forgive us and pick us up once again. He is a Mighty God. Thank you for dying on the cross for us all, making forgiveness possible.

It was time for me to get rid of the beauty shop.

Jesus showed me it was time to move on. Well, I needed a job, and I found one at another shop near my home.

I loved working with hair and meeting new people all the time. The owner of this shop wanted me to watch over the shop and the other workers to ensure they would not steal. She did not want to make me a manager but wanted me to work as one. I said no because I was one of them, just a worker, and she did not want to pay me for it.

Time went on and the customers that came in and had their hair done got to like me. I really do not understand what happened after this. But the owner's daughter came in with her mom and starting accusing of me trying to run the shop. I said that was not true, and her mom wanted me to be in charge, which I turned down.

My boss's daughter would not listen to me and started screaming at me. I tried to defend myself, but she did not want to listen to me, fired me right there, and threw me out of the building. I knew she was high on something, so I just left.

I was worried because I needed a job to take care of the house and family. So, I prayed and went out looking for a job.

The shop from where I was fired was sold to one of the other workers that was there. This person called me one day and rehired me. She was brand new in this field, so I helped her to learn the business.

Other workers were hired but became jealous of me. I was not sure why; maybe because I worked so hard. I had to; I had a family to take care of. And I believe in working unto Jesus and doing a good day's work. They were so spiteful, breaking my equipment and lying to my customers to take them away from me so they could do their hair. I thought to myself, *If they only really knew me, they would see that I had no confidence in my work at all.* I was never satisfied with my work; I strived to get better at each hairdo I did. I wanted every customer to walk out happy when they looked in the mirror at themselves. I was an okay hairdresser; I just tried hard to give the customers what they paid for.

It hurt me very much all the crazy things they did to me, but as I was talking to my friend, she asked me a question: "Why are you here?" As I thought about it, I realized I was here for Jesus to spread His Word. When the realization hit me, my hurt was gone. I was filled with much peace and joy. I continued to work there for fourteen years, a job that Jesus blessed me with.

Eventually, it was time for this owner to sell the shop. I was not sure if this was God's will for me or not, so I tried to purchase it. I went to the bank and took out a loan for it. Well, someone came that night to the owner and gave her cash for the shop, so I believed it was not God's will for me to own and be tied down to this shop. Jesus wanted me to be free and go wherever He needed me.

Well, here we are with a new boss. I knew I was here to make Jesus real to him. I enjoyed working there; he was very funny and made me laugh a lot. One day, his wife came in with a bad nosebleed. I had never seen a nosebleed so bad; the blood was just pouring from her nose. I asked if I could pray for her, and she said, "No, get away from me." But her husband, my boss, said yes. It was a simple prayer for Jesus to touch her and stop the bleeding, and as soon as I prayed, the bleeding stopped. My boss was so touched by this miracle that he just looked at me. I knew at that moment Jesus's presence was so strong he could not deny it, and God won his heart.

We never know where He will use us because Jesus knows everyone's heart condition. I was so happy to have the opportunity to be used in this life.

12
God's Love

I had a dream one night of an older gentleman who was to come into my life. He would be in the Mafia and wore old plain clothes and sneakers; you would have never guessed he was a godfather. I saw him in a limousine with my brother. He was a rough character, and I did not like him; he just was not my type of person. The dream was so vivid that I never forgot it, and it took five years to come to pass. One day, I remembered that I would meet him soon. I kept on checking the spirit to make sure this was of God because, to me, this was all wrong, but many things in that dream were coming to pass.

I went to a store with my older sister, and a man was working there. The Lord said, "This is the man I was telling you about." Well, he came over to me and started talking to me. He asked me to go to lunch, and I hesitated but said yes.

We became friends, and it lasted for many years until his death. I knew this man needed Jesus; the longer we were friends, the more I could see how much he needed the Lord. What a tortured soul he was. He was very good to my family and me, but he was an old-fashioned godfather for many years. I wanted nothing to do with this; I was there to bring him Jesus, and I told him so. He never involved me or my family in his work, which he respected. He never had any peace in his line of work, but I felt there was more to it. He had bad health as well.

As the years went by, I could see how Satan was destroying him, as he wanted to do to all of us. I was there to shine the light of Jesus, and he would say, "I never met a person like you before. You are like the other side of a coin." We would go out to eat, see plays, walk in the park, and sit at the beach. We never talked of his business, but I could see it in his face—we enjoyed the simple things in life.

I did not like all the things he did or how he spoke, but Jesus said, "Do not fight with him; he is used to that. Just show love and patience, which I would lose sometimes. He always watched me closely because that type of person trusts no one. I believe that is why Jesus chose me to represent Him in this man's life. I am quite gentle, loving, and trusting. He even tapped my phone and house for my protection and his. I did not care. I had nothing to hide. He was always worried someone was going to hurt me, but I trusted Jesus to take care of me. Any little mark on me, he would flip out of worry. He had little patience, a lot of fear, and a bad temper. Jesus used my household, because all he could hear were sermons of Him all day long. I was not interested in anything else; I was in love with Jesus.

What a wonderful God we have, for when yet we were sinners, He died for us. Here was a man of great sin who needed Jesus, and He waited patiently for him to receive such a great gift of salvation. He was fighting a disease that could not be cured, and he took his own life in the end. I cannot say he got saved because I do not know, but I know he lost his mind at the end of his life. No doctor or medicine could help him, only Jesus.

He made a statement for me to put in my book; he was sorry, for it was only business. I knew he meant what he said because he always chose his words carefully. I prayed he called unto Him at the end of his life. I will know when I get to heaven; my heart went out to him with the love Jesus placed in it for him. Jesus woke me up one night and said he was gone. Sorrow filled my heart, but Jesus comforted me and taught me a great lesson through it all: how great is His love for all mankind that He died on the cross. Sometimes, we get so self-righteous, but while I was yet a sinner, He saved me, so who am I to judge? God knew his heart.

I love you, Jesus.

13
Loneliness

The children were grown up now, and the house was too much for me to afford, so I had to sell it. It was hard for me to sell the house because of the memories that were there. We had a lot of fun together in this beautiful house. I had to know that this move was what God wanted. So, I kept on praying and asking Jesus for wisdom on what to do. I was behind in my real estate taxes, and I did not want to lose the house, so I believed this was one way God used for us to move. One day, a buyer came and gave me the cash and the price I asked for. I knew now it was time to move on to my next job for Jesus.

I have always loved the country with trees all around me. So, I moved far out on the Island to a retirement community. I was not old enough for this community, but they accepted me. I built a prefab home that looked like a doll house. I loved my little prefab home; it had two bedrooms and two bathrooms, plus a wood-burning fireplace, just right for me. For the first time in my life, I would be living alone. It had everything in it, including a fireplace that I loved. I would sit in front of it and read. It was such a wonderful blessing.

Something went wrong with the fireplace, and I did not know that the smoke was backing into my house. I fell asleep and could not wake up. The phone was ringing, and I woke up so sick. The person on the phone heard that I did not sound well, and they realized that something was wrong. They said to open the windows and doors, close the fireplace, and get out of the house. The smoke was so bad that my walls, which were once white, went black all the way to the back of the house. After that smoke, they were so dirty that a cleaning crew had to come in and wash everything: walls, rugs, the works.

My girlfriend came to visit me and saw the mess. She knew a fireplace owner and called him for me. He checked the situation and contacted the builder and had them repair it. Wow, God took care of me again, as I was never aware of the danger I was in.

I found a job on a school bus as an aide. The bus I was on was for children with behavioral problems. I had to keep my eyes open at all times to make sure they did not hurt me or the bus driver.

These children came from problem homes; some had parents who took drugs, and others were physically or sexually abused. Most of their parents were in jail, and their grandparents raised them. It seemed to me they were lost in the system at school. They were very hardcore for such a young age. They did not trust people at all; after all they had been through, I did not blame them.

I loved them with all my heart and wanted to be there for them. So, I started out on a quest to help them see real love and caring. They were very violent and not disciplined at all. Their clothes were unkept, and they were very unruly in every respect.

They could barely read or write and did not know what a report card was for. This just broke my heart, for I love children very much. They ranged in ages from five to eleven years old. But to me, they looked like they lived a lifetime already.

I prayed to see how to reach these children, God's children; how He loved them enough to send me there. Well, the first thing to do was to get them to behave and not fight or carry on so unruly. I decided to reward their behavior after each day with small gifts like lollipops, which they greatly appreciated; you would have thought I gave them something expensive. They were grateful for the small things I did for them; it made me see they were starving for love. They acted like they never had a piece of candy; it worked out great. They started to warm up to me and see that I really cared about them. Children know when someone really cares; they can see a phony from miles away.

I would read different children's books to them, on the way home and to school, to see how much they knew. Which was not too much; because they were in special classes, they did not know what grades were or report cards. So, we started reading, and I told them if they got a good report card, they would get a special surprise at the end of each week. And I always kept my promises to them. I told them if they did really well for Christmas, they would receive a nice gift from me.

I just gave from my heart, and they responded with open arms to me. If they were in trouble, they ran to me, and I would work it out for them. The workers were not allowed to touch the children; that was a school rule, but these children would run into my arms for a hug. It was so hard for me to restrain myself and not hug them back. Word got around about how I worked with the children in the school; if the school needed help, they would call me. I was not aware of what was happening, but the school would put me on different buses to control the kids, and it worked.

I was just an instrument of God's love, and children know who is sincere. They would tell me about their home life, and I would see their needs and try to help by asking people to help them with clothes, food, etc. It moved me so to see their hurts and broken hearts because of their difficult home environment. They did not trust anyone, and I was so moved by their tender love toward me.

One special little person attacked his teacher, and they put him away for six months in a special school specifically for children with behavior problems. I loved him so much and would pray for him a lot. In prayer, God told me to tell him that Jesus loves him. He just looked at me with tears in his eyes. The next week, he got on the bus and said to me, "I asked my grandma to take me to church, and I gave my heart to Jesus." I was so taken aback by this; he was a different child than before, happy, funny, loving, and responsive like never before. I was on that bus for about three years. His other five siblings were on the same bus. His sister never talked the whole time, and I used to sit on the seat next to her. She would come on the bus with wet pants every day.

Then, one day, I said to the bus driver, "She is wet all the way to her feet." I was so upset to see that she was sent to school this way. I was surprised when she spoke out for the first time; she said her dad would not clean her because water costs too much money. That was the beginning of a close friendship with her. She would not sit with anyone else or talk to them, either. The school investigated this and took care of it all.

On Halloween, we stopped the bus to let the children off, and a pickup truck smashed the back of the bus in. The children were in seat belts, but I was not because we stopped, and I was handing out candy. The impact of the pickup truck threw me into the front window of the bus. The children were fine, thank God. The police came, and you had to see the look of fear on their faces. The police had to question them, and the children would not answer them; God only knows what these children saw at home. I wanted to answer for them but was not allowed, so each time they addressed a child, I had to assure the child it was okay and safe. It was a sad scene to behold.

There was another young boy on the bus with us. He would talk to me about strange topics. I thought he was watching too much television, so I just ignored what he said. As the days went on, he got more and more serious and started crying. He wanted me to sit next to him, but my bus driver reminded me not to do that. So, I sat across from him, and he held my hand across the aisle.

He was crying a lot and said he did not want to be involved in what he was doing. I did not know what he was talking about, so I just listened to him. I was worried about him but did not understand what he was talking about, so I went to my boss and told him. But it was too late to help him because his family moved the next day. I still keep him in prayer. God knows his heart and where he is right now.

I did not know people were watching me so closely and seeing how much the children changed. It was a pleasure to see the results of all the time spent with them. At the end when I had to leave them, the school gave me a gold pin award for my work. But to me, being with the children blessed me; it was my pleasure and reward in itself, and it filled my loneliness.

I would love to see these children again someday, especially that young boy. I know God had a special place for them, for children are the apple of Jesus' eye. I would like to see how I made a difference in their lives.

One day, I was leaving school, and I was praying, as I always did on the way home. I stopped at a red light, thinking and listening to my worship and praise music. The light turned green, but in my spirit, I felt not to move, so I just sat there at that green light. Within a matter of seconds, a large 18-wheeler truck went through the red light. I thanked God that I listened to Him not to move because the truck would have hit me, and I would be dead. I thanked Him for His protection and thought about how many times He had taken care of me that I was not aware of. What a mighty God we serve.

I also worked as a hairdresser in the community to make some money to support myself. I had many elderly customers, and my heart went out to them. They never seemed to have any company, so as I did their hair, I would also visit with them. As I got to know them, I saw they did not eat well, so I would cook extra and bring them some food.

They were very lonely and did not see their family much; I would check on them to make sure they were alright and even would food shop for them. I felt in my heart that I was the only one they would see Jesus in right now, and I loved doing it. It brought much joy to my heart. I continued to live there for another three years.

As this friendship grew with the elderly, I would talk to them about Jesus, because a lot of times, I was the last one they saw before they died. They would ask me to do their hair when they died because I knew how they liked to wear it. They would share all their hurts and about their life. I enjoyed listening to them; it was very interesting to hear about the past. After their deaths, sometimes I would write a little note to the families and tell them how much they were loved.

I love to share God's love because I know what He did for me and how He loves everyone by sending His Son to die at Calvary for our sins.

Sometimes people forget about the elderly and the young, but they need love, as all of us do. They are worth it if we would take the time and stretch out a loving hand.

It is a sad world with lots of lonely people in it, so give a helping hand when you can, or give a smile; it can go very far in this life. You never know what another person has been through that day. If we would only open our hearts to Jesus, He will lead us into this world to be His hand of kindness, helping others in the time of need. Someday, it may be our turn to need this helping hand.

I loved helping people and talking to them about Jesus.

One of my elderly hair customers was a retired Army General. He called for me to give him a haircut because he was going to die soon. As I went into his room, He said to me, "Will you please sit down?" and asked his wife to leave the room.

As I sat there, he started to talk to me about his

life and sicknesses. As I listened, my heart hurt for him. He said the doctors wanted to remove his legs, and he did not want to live that way. So, he stopped his dialysis, and he would be dead soon. I was very taken aback by what he was confiding in me. He was a general who could not face life with no legs. I sat and prayed while he spoke to me about Jesus and asked if God would be angry with him for not taking dialysis.

I spoke on God's forgiveness and mercy toward His little ones. I told him I was sure God understood that if He did not heal him, he wanted to die a natural death. I finished cutting his hair, and he laid down in his bed in peace. How good Jesus is to His people and knows every heart.

I was getting sicker and sicker with bronchitis and pneumonia four times a year, and it was difficult to work. I had to leave the bus job and those precious children.

When I left, they did not understand what happened to me and went back to their old habits and fears. The bus driver had to call me on a cellphone so I could talk to them and help them understand that I was sick and had to go. I was not letting them down, just very sick and had to go to Virginia to live with my daughter. They were not behaving for the new aide on the bus, and I was worried about them.

I love children and hate when they are abused in any form. They did not ask to come into this world, so their parents should take good care of them. And when they failed them, God, their heavenly Father, took care of them. I also love working with the elderly (Acts 20:35).

One day, I took my granddaughter to the beach, and we got lost. She turned around to me and said, "This is strange, grandma." I feel like God wanted us to meet someone at the beach, and Satan wanted to stop us. Why would we get lost when we have been there so many times?

We saw an ice cream truck and bought some ice cream. I thought the truck looked odd, and I had an uneasy feeling about the owner. He came and sat next to us on a bench. We had a light conversation about the world and life. Then, his tone grew more aggressive as we talked about where he came from.

He said he traveled a lot around the world and did odd jobs. He said that he hated Jewish people, and that is why he hated Americans, because we love them. I was praying the whole time, asking Jesus to give me the right words for this hate-stricken man.

I started to talk about the love of God and how He puts that love in our hearts for all mankind. This man was talking about killing both Jews and

Americans. Satan was making him get very angry, but I would not back down. Jesus had filled me with wisdom on what to say to him.

My words touched this man's heart, because he started to listen to me with a calm spirit. This was nobody but Jesus because, at first, I thought he would hurt us, and I was afraid for my granddaughter's safety. When I left that man sitting on the bench, he just stared at me with peace in his heart. To this day, I still pray for him to get to know Jesus; I hope I planted a seed of love. Jesus showed me His love for this man and how He loved all mankind, even though we were yet sinners.

14
The Move

I loved my little house and did not want to move, but money was getting tight, and my health was going downhill. One day, I had very bad pneumonia with a high fever. I had slept for days and did not leave my house. My neighbor became concerned about not seeing me outside. She came to my house and was knocking on my door to see if I was okay. It took a while for me to answer the door, for my fever was so high I was delirious. She kept on knocking harder each time, and finally, she woke me. She took one look at me and took me to the hospital right away. It was getting more challenging to get better. I knew by then I had to slow down so I could fight getting sick so often. I felt this was God's way of pushing me to move.

I did much praying and laid many metaphorical fleeces before Him to confirm this move. One of the prayers was for Him to send a Christian buyer, and I charged a high price for the house. I did leave it fully furnished with brand-new furniture, so I did not feel guilty about the price. Plus, I kept the house very clean; it was practically brand new.

He not only sent a Christian but a pastor. The pastor said, "I can get this house cheaper, but God said to give you this price and in cash." Now I knew what I was to do: move and live with my daughter and her family. I had to know that a change of this magnitude was truly of God. He met all my requirements, and I could not deny His request.

Well, I was on my way to a new adventure in life. I knew it was getting close to retirement, but not just yet. First things first, I needed a job. Where to start? Let's pray for Jesus' guidance once more. It was time to move out of my comfort zone again. Not just a job but a new place of worship.

My daughter and her family and I found old friends when we arrived, although we did not know they lived there until after we had arrived. God had a perfect plan; we just stepped out in faith, trusting Him, leaving all our family, friends, and all we knew behind us and went to the land He called us to.

Our friends showed us around the city, suggested places to live, and invited us to their church. We moved here on absolute, complete faith. We recognized this was home as things started falling into place, and we felt God's leading as we all prayed for His guidance and will.

It was a nice church for us, and we fit right in and felt at home. Little by little, we realized who the pastor was, and we knew his family from New York, as his father preached in our old church. What a small world.

A vision God showed me years before started to materialize with this Pastor, and I knew God put us here. I knew we were on the right path because the devil was mad. He tried to hit us with many things, from money issues to sickness and so on. But this church was an advocate of prayer and fasting, which I did with my family and with which we broke the chains. I give thanks and praise to God because what Satan tried to use to destroy this family, God used for good.

We continued to attend this church, and we settled in to life in this new city. I watched the past hurts and hang-ups within me slowly dissolve away. I could feel the chains that bound me melting away, and my heart grew lighter so Jesus could use me once again.

Jesus sent me a very good job with a Christian boss in a coffee shop, which I took care of and loved. I needed a job because my money was very low. It was a perfect job for me, being around people again.

I grew better, stronger, and more mature by learning from my past to trust Jesus and not man. No matter what happens in life, I wanted to get better, not bitter. When you are bitter, it hurts you physically and mentally. It damages the body and makes you sick. It will hurt your walk with God by blocking your prayer life and harden your heart against receiving God's love.

We must all make our own choices. Jesus took me by the hand and lead me through a successful life that I could not create on my own.

Looking back at my life, at times I listened to Satan's lies, which I thought were real. Instead of trusting Jesus, I got lost in problems. I wrongly put my eyes on people when they should have been on God. I am so glad that Jesus was so patient with me, as so many times I had to learn the same lessons over and over again.

There will always be problems; the difference is Jesus carries you through them. And we learn by these experiences how real and close He is to us. Plus, He knows the beginning of our lives to the end and wants to grow closer to us and us to Him. He never leaves you or gives up on you. Jesus is a gentleman; He will not make you do something like Satan does, lying to you. He will gently guide you, but you must make the final decision out of your love for Him.

There will be ups and downs, good and bad. In Him, your joy will be complete, for happiness comes from your heart within, not from the outside world. That kind of joy is brief. Like buying something, it brings joy for the moment, but then it gets old, and you need to buy something else. Your final peace comes from within, where Jesus reigns; He will lead and guide you throughout your life. The final decision you make to serve Jesus is yours and yours alone.

I always have questions about my walk with the Lord, and I continually went before Him, searching my heart to make sure it was pure before Him. I want to be an instrument of His love, not my own motives. I still was not satisfied with the situation in my first church, and I sought the Lord on it once again. Jesus is always right, but was I doing what He wanted of me, being just flesh and blood? I always try to stay before Him so my flesh does not overcome me. Only by leaning on Him can we stay on this narrow road ahead, knowing that it is possible through the cross Of Christ.

There was a visiting speaker at our new church, and at this time, I asked the Lord to reassure me once again through the church service. There was a prayer line, and I joined it, wanting God to touch me that evening. As the pastor prayed over me, I was slain in the Holy Spirit like never before. I could not get off the floor or speak in English for four hours, and Jesus renewed my inner man.

That was not the only thing. This pastor had a Bible study program that I was very interested in, but it was too expensive for me to purchase. As I went to the foyer after the service, a young woman from our church whom I did not know approached me and offered to buy it for me as a gift. She insisted on getting this for me; she said Jesus told her to.

The study was on God's word throughout the Bible, and I loved it. As I completed this course, Jesus revealed to me that I was completely knowledgeable in His Word, and I walked in it. It was His work He called me to, and I did it, but I was not sure if I did it right. I was never sure what exactly went wrong in my past, but I know it was His leading that used me there, not my own. In my old church, there was much said against me, and I did not want to be used anymore if I was doing wrong.

I knew my life was in God's hands (Job 12). I never thought that I was a person who could write a book. As you can see, I am not much of a writer. At the beginning, I felt like Moses, who did not feel up to the task that the Lord asked him to do. However, I knew I had to be obedient. To obey is better than sacrifice.

I know now, through much prayer, that Jesus chose me because He spoke to me when I got saved and told me that I would have to choose the road He prepared for me so I may testify of His great love for us. Sometimes, it did not seem that way, but hindsight is a great teacher. I am not perfect, just forgiven. Jesus will perfect the work He started in me until the end of my days when He calls me home. All I can do is walk on His path of life and praise Him in the good times and the bad. Jesus brought hope in my heart again, and I praise Him and thank Him for it.

Perhaps you don't see any purpose in your life yet, but then He isn't finished making you. And besides, you may be arguing with the process.

If you would only believe they are still in the process of creation, submit to the Maker, allow Him to handle them as the potter handles the clay, and yield yourself in one shining, deliberate action to the turning of His wheel, you would soon find yourself able to welcome every pressure from His hand, even if it results in pain. And sometimes you should not only believe but also have God's purpose in sight, bringing many sons to glory (Heb.2:10).

NOT A SINGLE BLOW CAN HIT
TILL THE GOD OF LOVE SEES FIT.

I learned something from the assistant pastor of my old church, a very wise man. When the Holy Spirit leads you to do something, do not go back and examine it, then or in the future. I just wanted to work for Jesus, no matter what it was—serve people, clean the church, cook, visit the shut-ins, etc. I was willing to do anything to bring Jesus' Word to people.

Throughout this wonderful course, I was able to see more clearly who God is and who I am. This course took me out of religious hurt and into a much closer walk with Jesus. I learned at a deeper level the importance of reading the Word and studying to show myself approved.

As my walk continued, I began to realize my authority in Christ. I have begun to overcome my past hurts from a very challenging life. I came to realize that I can truly tread on "snakes" and "scorpions" and not be defeated, and I have learned that when I have done all to stand, just stand and wait on Jesus to deliver you.

One day, I was food shopping, and my funds were low. I was walking through the store with a song of Jesus in my heart. A precious lady was in the same aisle. She approached me and started talking to me about how Jesus told her to talk to me. We talked and prayed together for a long time. She talked about her husband, who was a

Christian but lived like the devil. She was very hurt by him, and I told her to pray for him because God wishes no man to perish. She did not like my answer. But I knew that was the answer God told me to say, and she went away sad. I pray someday she understands that answer.

Before she left, she said Jesus told her to give me money for food. I did not want to take it, but she insisted. I did not want to offend her, so I took the money. As we departed, I could not thank her enough for this blessing. Again, I saw God's hand provide for me from a woman I had never seen before. I think of her quite often and pray for the many needs of her family. I know that Jesus is going to answer her prayers one day. She filled my heart with such great love. I was overwhelmed by her generosity.

I draw nigh to Him daily and resist the devil. Although temptation would come my way, I turned to the Word or listened to preaching CDs to reinforce the Word in my heart. I realize that I must continually walk in my heavenly identity and authority at all times, because the devil is walking about like a hungry lion, seeking whomever he can devour.

I love to read God's word; it is as honey to my lips and healing balm to my soul. I am learning to live and act on the word of God, and I see that as I walk through the doors that God leads me through, these are doors that no man can shut. I find that I walk closer with God; he infused me with strength; He's my rock, my strong tower, and my shield (Psalm 91). My favorite Bible chapter for all my family, each day I would place on their beds a Bible open to this verse.

We must realize that each day of our lives is one day closer to heaven if we stay in His Word daily. You can go to heaven or bring heaven to earth by living the Word, not just reading it. The road to heaven is narrow, but the road to hell is wide open, so we must be on our guard to seek Him every day with an open heart. My dad had a saying that many people make God in THEIR own image. I did not want to be one of them. I wanted to be made in His image so people may see Him through me.

One day I came down with shingles even though I received the shingles vaccine. I had a bad case of it, and my doctor was quite concerned. We were both worried about my lungs because I have asthma; if they were to become infected also, I might not have made it through. Well, God was not finished with me yet.

My doctor gave me medication for the shingles, hoping it would help me, even though you are to take this medication within twenty-four hours of the first sign of the sickness.

I did not know I had the shingles, because a few days earlier, I hurt my back really bad and could not move. Then I saw the sores on my body and went to see the doctor. It was four days later, and there was a good chance that this medication would not work. My doctor said, "Let's take a chance; you may get a miracle." And I did.

Not realizing this medication would make me so sick, I became frightened and started to pray for Jesus' help. The medication made me hallucinate, vomit, gave me diarrhea, and kept me from sleeping. It was so severe I lost ten pounds in two weeks. The doctor could not give me certain medication to help me because of my asthma. When you have asthma and you take sleep medication, you can sleep so deeply that you may not wake up. The doctor wanted me to continue the medication, hoping it could still help, because shingles can stay in your body for years with a lot of nerve pain. Better to be sick this way than for years to come.

I did not want to be left alone, so my granddaughter slept in my room with me. I could not sit, stand, or sleep; I would pace the house all day and night long. There was no relief at all, just applying ice, which was not so good because I was ice cold all the time. I went to the bathroom so much I would pass out, and my family was so worried. What made it worse for me was that, due to the medicine, I knew that I was acting crazy and could not help myself.

All night long, I would pray and listen to sermons from the Bible. They strengthened my faith and brought me closer to Jesus. I stood on His Word that I was going to be okay and I would make it through, and I did. Something happened at this time; my best friend, who lives four hours away, got shingles at the same time. We laughed together about it, and she said she got it from me over the phone. I thanked God for the recovery we both received and how Jesus took care of us both (2 Corinthians 1:3-4). I could not understand what the medication did. I thought I was losing my mind. One day, a nurse told me that her dad had the same reaction to his medication. Wow, that helped me feel better.

I have many Bibles in my house. As I aged, my eyesight got worse, so I had to get a Bible that I could see better. I looked through my old Bibles and saw what I had written in them, all different seasons of my life. I could see where I came from, where I am today, and how I grew, which encouraged me. The Scripture verses that I underlined and the little notes I put next to them helped to lighten my path and build my faith.

When I was raising my children, there were many sleepless nights wondering if they were alright. Not until I went on my knees and prayed for peace, like every God-fearing parent, did sleep come. I was always talking to Jesus and asking questions about life. At those times, He would send me an encouraging word through people or His Word, or someone would send me a word.

My close friend bought a book for me that Jesus led her to buy. The book's title is "The Flames Shall Not Consume You" by Mary Ellen Ton. It documents how the author was burned in a fire while working at her husband's office. It was on the second floor, and she had to jump from the window. She was severely burned over most of her body. This book touched my heart so deeply and healed my mind from Satan's lies. To see someone who has been through so much in life! The author shared her hopes, dreams, and insecurities, and it touched me so heavily that I cried. It was as if she was writing about me or for me. I shared her hurts and pain in thinking my outward appearance was the most important thing in the world.

I was a short, fat girl with thick glasses, and people made fun of me a lot. My mom tried her best to assure me that I was pretty, but her way was not God's way. She meant well, but she believed that our bodies were what made us who we are, which is not true. It is our inner man, our heart.

That is the world's way of seeing things. The world places a heavy emphasis on our appearance. That is for narrow-minded, shallow people. God looks for what is in our heart. He sees the heart's intent and knows our motives. Jesus does not judge the book by its cover as the world does. That is why only He can judge each life.

For many months, the author struggled with self-pity, fear, anger, and loneliness. However, she uncovered her true identity, the identity God loved that was deep down inside, smothered by ashes but not overcome. This is where she found her self-esteem.

God has many resourceful ways to let us know we are on the right path and loved. I think I wore out the pages from the many times I have read this book because it spoke right to me. It hurt to see my shortcomings and how He put this all together for me to understand how we all hurt sometimes, and it is okay not to be ashamed of myself.

He said in His Word, "Then I went into the sanctuary, and I understood" (Psalm 73:17). It was there that I understood what He was telling me and what to do with it: glorify Him.

What an honor it is to talk about God the Father, Jesus the Son, and the Holy Spirit. For it is His Holy Spirit that guides us into all truth, allowing us to open up and worship our Lord and Savior with spirit and truth.

Start praising and worshiping Him. See how mighty our God really is and how much He loves us. It is through worship that we hear His still, small voice. Listen and obey it, for we only pass this way once, and then eternity comes, so don't miss a second to spend time with Him. Do not let any opportunity pass you by. You never know what is ahead.

Leaving New York and going so far away, I missed my sisters very much. God gave me a dream of my older sister lying in a hospital bed in a red living room. I was sitting next to her, holding her hand. She was wearing a dark blue dress, and she looked very sick.

Being so far away, I had not been to her house for a year. I did not know what her new home was like. I put this dream out of my mind, saying it was just a dream, not really real.

I went to her house about two weeks later to visit her, and her living room was painted red. I said, "This is odd," and left the thought alone. She started to feel sick one day as we were shopping, our favorite pastime. I said to her, "Please go to the doctor; maybe it is just a stomach virus," but she would not go. She had pain in her lower stomach, and the pain was growing stronger. The pain was getting more severe, so she finally went to her doctor.

She did not like doctors; she believed they just wanted money, and she would never go for check-ups. When we finally talked her into going, it was too late. The doctor did all he could, but the cancer was too far along in her body. They said she did not have much time to live, only a few weeks.

The whole family was in shock, to say the least. I worried about my dad very much. He was in his nineties now, and to see a child die before he did really hurt. Hospice care was called into the house to take care of her because she did not want to die in the hospital. The hospice nurse told us that day that she would die in a few hours, so I called my dad and asked him if he wanted to say his last goodbyes to her.

He was so overwhelmed that my son had to carry him from the car into the house to see her. Her sons came from all over the country to see her for the last time, and we all gathered around her, praying and asking God for help to comfort her. Her son and husband, who were taking care of her, were so good and gentle with her.

I stood with them the whole event and asked

Jesus to give me strength for her five boys' sake. People from the church came and prayed with her; the peace of God was greatly in this home.

Then the dream God gave me came back to my mind, that Jesus was preparing me and the family by letting us know that He was here with us. That dark blue dress in the dream was the same blue dress she was buried in, the dress she wore to her son's wedding.

Before she passed, I sat next to her and held her hand, and she would ask me about dying. She asked me if she was really going to die now and told me she did not want to leave her sons and husband. I did all I could not to break down in front of her. I waited until I left her, and then I could not stop crying, for the pain in my heart was so great there were no words to explain my feelings.

We do not always understand His ways, but let us put our trust in Him, because I was numb and in shock about this whole thing. I loved my sister and miss her very much, but I know she is in a better place with no pain or worry. Someday, I will see her, mom, dad, my husband and all my loved ones in Heaven. What a day of rejoicing that will be!

I went back to my home, and in my room alone, I would pray for Jesus to help me with my weak areas and make me strong. There were areas of pain to be healed in me and areas of pride to surrender so that He may shine through a yielded vessel, holy and pure in His sight. My heart loves God, but my flesh had to come under subjection and obedience to His Word. I wanted to be more like Jesus, so I would read all about Him in the Bible and then obey His Word. Only He can transplant our hearts.

Jesus has used me many times to speak to people just before they die or to help the family throughout their time of mourning. I was not sure why He chose me for this. I think it is one of the most painful times in people's lives. Sometimes, there are no words to help. You just have to be there for them and listen while you pray for them.

There is a song I like to sing, "To Be More Like Him". To be more like Him, we must die to our flesh and rise up to become more in the image of Jesus. My heart's desire is to be like Jesus. I still vividly remember the day He appeared to me, the Love in His eyes. I want His love in me so I may be able to touch those around me in my little corner of the world.

I was learning to trust Jesus more and more. I was not sure why we were sent to move, and I found out one of the reasons was there was a great eye doctor who had the courage to deal with my eyesight.

I had spent my whole life seeing doctors, and no one wanted to help me see better. They were afraid to take a chance, as I had one blind eye. I had gone to many doctors all over New York, and no one would help me.

When we first moved, I had no job or money. I had to go to a free clinic for help. They were such great people and took good care of me. They did everything there, dentistry, eyes, and medical and medication, all free.

I was so thankful because I came down with bad asthma, and the medication was very expensive. The doctors were so good and careful with me; they would take me in right away so I did not sit with sick people or I would become sicker. My son found this clinic for me on the internet, praise God.

It was time for an eye exam, and they scheduled me for a check-up. I thought to myself, *Here we go again; another doctor who will tell me how bad my eyes are and there is nothing he can do for me.*

For the first time in my life, this doctor said to me, "Yes, your eyes are very bad. But when the time comes, I will operate on them and, if need be, for nothing." What a shock that was, not just that he would operate but that he would do it for nothing. He said, "I never worked on such bad eyes before, but I believe I can fix them."

I was so overwhelmed I was speechless. I was born with very poor vision, very near-sighted. One eye was legally blind, and when I applied for a driver's license, I could not take the eye test; I would bring a note from the doctor.

A few years passed, and I went to this doctor for regular eye exams. He said I had cataracts, and they were ready to be removed. He said he would also put implants in, so I would be able to see with no glasses. No more thick glasses or contacts. Unbelievable, because other doctors said this could not be done, that even contacts would hurt my eyes. I was the only one in my family with such bad vision. My prescription was minus 20 in my right eye and minus 17 in my left eye, and I still was not able to see very well.

The day came for the operation, and my daughter took me to the hospital. One eye went with no trouble; I was out of the operating room in 20 minutes. The doctor sat me up in a chair and said, "What do you see across the room?" I could see clearly as a bell for the first time in my life. I saw a lady across the room with short black hair lying in a bed. Praise God. What seemed so strange was that I was the youngest person there for such an operation; the nurse there came over and told me this.

The second eye, my bad one, took 40 minutes in the operating room. My daughter was very worried because an asthma patient was not supposed to be put in a deep sleep; they do not always wake up. The reason it took so long was the doctor had to put the lens in manually, not with an instrument; it would not work. Well, today, for the first time in my life, I can get up in the morning and do not have to reach for my glasses to see. I have 20/40 vision, and for the first time in my life, I can see a leaf on a tree and the beauty of a snowflake or flower. I cannot express my joy in being able to see. I lay in bed in the morning and looked around my room at the swirls in my ceiling, thinking how pretty they are.

When I stopped to think about my eyes, I remember I prayed for God to heal them about thirty years ago. He did not forget His promise to me. I do not know why He waited so long. Maybe I needed a blessing so great at *this* time of my life.

However, I have a new eye condition that just occurred. I am seventy years old now, and both my eyes are afflicted with macular degeneration. The night before I had an eye doctor's appointment, the Lord Jesus told me to pray for my doctor tomorrow because I would be witnessing to Him; this would be my first visit to this doctor. So I did pray and went to sleep. As I lay in bed, I thought, *What an odd request from Him.*

I went to the doctor the next day, and he checked my eyes. Then he turned to me and said, "I do not know how you see so well. Your eyes are so bad, I do not understand how you are seeing at all." His whole staff was in the room with me, about six people. I guess he needed help to tell me this. He continued to tell me there was no hope for me, that I would go blind. There is no medicine or needles that will help.

At that moment, Jesus reminded me that I was to testify to him. It just came out, like I was floating on a cloud, that my hope was in Jesus, not in man, and that He would heal me. The doctor was getting off his chair to leave, so he stopped, turned, and looked at me as if to remember something. He said, "That is right." There was such a presence of Jesus in that room that I just wanted to pray and thank Him for that encouraging word. I am 75 now and still see good; praise Him for this miracle.

I love living in the South; it is a slower pace of life here, which I needed in my body at this time. I had lived at such a fast pace, always trying to take care of the children's needs by working hard. I never took time off, not even when I was very sick with a fever. I would go to the doctor for medication and not take time to rest; just go straight to work. I remember one doctor said to me, "Slow down; you are not a brain surgeon." That was true, but I had four kids and a household to take care of. I needed the money, so I could not miss any work at all. Plus, my boss would get really mad at me. One day, I wanted to see my son's new baby, and when I asked to leave early, he threatened to fire me.

The work was hard on my body; standing in one place all day, plus breathing in the fumes from the chemicals, was hurting my lungs. For about forty years, I worked this way, including side jobs. Some days, I worked from eight in the morning to eleven at night. I would fall into bed exhausted; working six days a week did not help me at all. And some people are very nasty, and that would hurt me, because I try so hard to do right.

One day, I was so tired when I came home from work that I sat at the end of my bed and just fell over and went to sleep. The next day, I woke up in the same spot and wondered what happened to me. I never got in my bed, just fell over and slept at the edge of my bed. I do believe that I did not take good care of myself; wearing my body down like that made my immune system weaken. I was not able to fight back colds or the flu; they would always turn into pneumonia.

My weakened immune system caused many upper respiratory infections, which were hard to heal because I was so run down. The doctors were quite concerned for my welfare. It was hard for them to help me because I was allergic to many medications, products around me, and the air in general. I had no one to help me, so I just asked Jesus and went on with life.

I had to start eating right, exercising, and getting plenty of rest. When I first got here, I slept ten hours a day, which was unusual for me. The change in climate brought on bronchitis, which turned into pneumonia, and eventually, I got a bad case of asthma. I suffered for many years with this, and the struggle has been great. I had to quit a part-time job because the attacks would come just from being around people. I decided if I stayed in my own element, just trying to build my body back up again, the asthma attacks were less frequent. There were fewer visits to the ER, and I was taking less medication. Plus, being sick all the time, the strain on my lungs was taking a physical toll on my body. It was very hard to leave my house or go visit someone or shop. I never knew what I was going to face beyond my room.

But I found that by taking good care of myself (which I never did), I am getting better and stronger each day; my doctor said I am doing great. I thank Jesus for directing me here because the doctors were so attentive to me. With their care and God's guiding hand, I am recovering very nicely. I will never run a marathon, but I can go outside again with no restrictions.

Like before, I could not go out because I was allergic to flowers, grass, and trees. I could not breathe at all; I felt like bugs were crawling all over me. I went for allergy shots, but I was so sick I was allergic to them as well. Then, I knew I had to depend on Jesus to heal me and make me whole.

I am doing very well now. Occasionally, I need to take maintenance medication. My breathing attacks are only a few. Sometimes, I want to get out of my environment and go on a vacation, but I do not feel ready yet. Every time I did that, I landed in the ER. I am hoping one day to be completely well.

It is hard to go somewhere and not know what kind of air is there. Will it bring on an asthma attack? That has happened so many times to me that I became afraid and very cautious about where I went, not only for me but for the people around me, who got scared, as well. Back then, not even the medicines were helping me. The doctor had to double my medications, which frightened me. Praise God, I am feeling so much better.

I can now walk around the neighborhood and get some exercise.

There are many hurting people in this world, and I hope I can encourage them with hope that Jesus is still on His throne. He will carry us through any storm in our lives, if we let Him. I pray within these pages there is hope and life for the hungry and rest for the weary.

Pray and open your heart and eyes to receive God's mighty power of love, healing, and health of mind, body, and soul. As I grow older, I can see all Jesus took me through and how He strengthened me. Time and time again, hindsight makes things so clear that I can see where He took me from and where I am today.

His grace and mercy have sustained me throughout my life's journey. Some people would say I could have dealt with these problems, but that is not the truth. Everyone knows him or herself the best. I know how weak I am and how strong He is. I know I cannot control anything in life. I was so messed up, and no earthly man could fix me. Only leaning on Jesus, for I know what He did for me. He is no respecter of persons; He loves us all no matter what or who we are. He took me out of the miry clay and planted my feet on the King's highway.

How many times do doubts cast their weird

shadows over us, doubts that life's best and choicest things are not over? But His Word can strengthen us and restore us. The blessed fact is that He still goes before us all the days of our lives.

When you are close to Jesus, He will take care of you and your family. I could not fix myself, but He cared enough to send His only begotten Son to die for us at Calvary when we were yet sinners. What a mighty God we serve! He will always watch over us no matter what, if we stay close to Him, within His love.

I am glad I was obedient to my heavenly Father and shared my life, putting it down on these pages so I may help my Christian sisters and brothers in Jesus.

My body is aging, as is all of us, but Jesus is still there for us. He still directs us to different doctors, places, and people. The peace and joy in my heart is in Him. Sometimes, I am healed completely in a miracle, and other times, He has sent me to a doctor for His glory to be a testimony that He is on the throne. He is not through with us yet, not until we get to heaven and are with Him.

Jesus has said, "Be still and know I am God." If we will only learn that lesson in life: to pray and then be still in trusting our Savior, Lord and King.

The Bible is truth; all His promises are alive

and real. He has put hope and joy in my heart, and I would like to reach into the world and share it with others. I want to cry out to all who will listen because I lived in this world of faith and belief in His Word. We need to live in childlike faith, for we are in the palm of His hand, and He knows all about our tomorrows.

15
Praise Him

I have learned to wait on God's timing in my life. I wrote this book 20 years ago, and now He allowed me to have it published. His timing is always perfect in our lives. I learned not to go ahead of Him because He knows what is best. Timing is a very important part of life, and too often, I can get impatient and want to move ahead of His way. I do not want to just sit quietly; it is not me. The Lord then reminds me to just rest in Him. I learned to listen to the still small voice and pray to wait on His further instructions because they are the best way, and I had to learn that, sometimes, the hard way. I am a doer and had to learn to slow down and rest in Him. My heart's desire is to be God's servant and submit my flesh in all things. It is all part of growing in my Heavenly Father.

I learned much about praying through problems, even when my flesh was hurting so badly. I ultimately left my problems in God's hands because He knows the beginning from the end, and

He knows our hearts.

I just wanted to be used for God's glory and stand behind the cross of Christ so He may be lifted up for the world to see. He did it for me; He can do it for you, too.

Because He lives, I can face TOMORROW!!!!!!

JESUS' FOREVER CHILD, I LOVE YOU LORD!

AMEN.

Printed in the USA
CPSIA information can be obtained
at www.ICGtesting.com
JSHW022256021024
70890JS00001B/5

9 781957 497396